31 Months in Japan

31 Months in Japan

The Building of a Theme Park

Larry K. & Lorna Collins

iUniverse, Inc.
New York Lincoln Shanghai

31 Months in Japan
The Building of a Theme Park

Copyright © 2005 by Lorna Collins

iUniverse books may be ordered through booksellers or by contacting:

iUniverse
2021 Pine Lake Road, Suite 100
Lincoln, NE 68512
www.iuniverse.com
1-800-Authors (1-800-288-4677)

ISBN-13: 978-0-595-34584-7 (pbk)
ISBN-13: 978-0-595-67133-5 (cloth)
ISBN-13: 978-0-595-79331-0 (ebk)
ISBN-10: 0-595-34584-0 (pbk)
ISBN-10: 0-595-67133-0 (cloth)
ISBN-10: 0-595-79331-2 (ebk)

Printed in the United States of America

Dedication

This book is dedicated to the USJ team—from America and Japan—whose efforts and determination created one of the greatest theme parks in the world—Universal Studios Japan.

And in Memory of

Raouf Iskander

Contents

Prologue

Theme Park
An amusement park in which the rides and attractions are built with a particular theme.
In the case of Universal Studios®[1] theme parks, the attractions are based on Universal films.

✶   ✶   ✶   ✶   ✶

Lorna

I was lost, thoroughly lost, in a country where I neither read the signs nor spoke much of the language. I was just trying to get to a dentist. The crown on my front tooth had fallen out the day before, and English-speaking friends had recommended their Harvard-trained doctor. I called his office and made an appointment for that afternoon. Then I boarded the train.

"Take the *JR* (Japan Railway) to *Amagasaki* where you'll catch the local to the *Koshienguchi* station in *Nishinomiya*," they'd said. What they hadn't told me was there were three different local trains as well as an express and a limited express heading that direction. Only one of them stopped at the specified station, and it wasn't the one I was on.

I spotted the name written in English as the train whizzed past, but couldn't get off until about three stations later when the car halted and the doors opened. I studied the schedules posted on the platforms, but at that point didn't recognize enough Japanese to figure out where I needed to go. And there were no other foreigners in sight.

Japanese business people and students rushed past me, staring as if I had just dropped in from another planet. They seemed curious, but too intimidated to offer help. Unlike me, they knew where they were going and how to get there.

I eventually found the platform where I could head back, but still didn't know which train to take. The first streaked past without stopping. The second

---

[1] Universal Studios and all ride and attraction names in this book are registered trademarks.

was too crowded. I finally gathered my courage and boarded the third, only to pass my targeted station again, this time going the opposite direction. Fortunately, I was able to get off just one station beyond my goal.

For a moment I considered walking, but there were no streets paralleling the tracks. Being lost on the train was bad enough. Getting thoroughly confused on foot would have been even worse.

Once again, I changed platforms. The next train that pulled in appeared to be smaller than the previous ones and more worn. Figuring perhaps they saved the older ones for the routes with more stops, I got on, nearly an hour late and hoping this time I'd guessed right. Fortunately I had, but I spent the walk to the office wondering what the heck I was doing in Japan instead of back home in California.

✳   ✳   ✳   ✳   ✳

The call that started it all came in March of 1997 from my best friend Pat who was working as contracts administrator for Universal Studios in Hollywood.

"Do you think Larry would be interested in working on the design for our new location in *Osaka*?"

Pat, Larry and I had all previously worked for the same engineering company. Larry was still there, but his office was being downsized. After nearly thirty years, he had begun to think about leaving.

"The position will require relocating to Japan during construction. How would you feel about living there for a couple of years?" she asked.

I had been interested in the Japanese culture for years. My friend, Kay, was born and raised in the port city of *Kobe* near *Osaka*, and we had previously hosted several Japanese students in our home.

I laughed confidently. "You forget we have 'kids' there. It's probably the foreign country I'd most like to see. Over the years I've learned so much, it would be great to finally experience it for myself."

"Well, the A&E (Architecture & Engineering) director, Tony, has been in my office all afternoon raging and ranting that he can't find anyone for a position he's trying to fill," Pat explained. "He's already interviewed a dozen people who sounded good on paper but weren't actually qualified. I asked him what experience he was looking for. He told me bluntly I couldn't possibly know anyone who would be adequate. So I dared him to describe the job to me anyway. He rattled off a long list of requirements, and it sounded like he was reading directly from Larry's resume. That's why I'm calling."

That night we discussed Larry's applying. He had worked on another theme park project a couple of years earlier and really enjoyed it, so he decided to submit his resume and see what developed.

Within a week, he was called for an interview, and it seemed like a perfect match. According to Tony, he was needed immediately and would be contacted shortly with an offer. March passed into April, then May and all the way into July with an occasional, "We're working on it," from Universal, but nothing tangible was forthcoming.

Meanwhile, Larry was approached about several other positions, all of which were clearly wrong for him. Then our friend Tom asked him to interview with his firm. The office was closer to home; the salary acceptable and it seemed like a good position. When he left for work the next day, it was his intention to accept.

At the time, it was our habit to eat lunch together on Fridays. Larry got off work at 11:30 and would come by my office to pick me up. When I got into the car that day, I asked, "Well, did you accept the job?"

I could tell by the look on his face, something was up. All he replied was, "Universal called."

In The Beginning...

Hashi (hah-shee)
Chopsticks. There are many kinds of hashi: those for eating meals, those used for cooking and those for picking up cakes and sweets. They are usually made of wood, but can also be found in ivory, bamboo and metal. They are often painted or decorated with designs.

*   *   *   *   *

Larry
Day One

I arrived at Universal Studios Hollywood, after my two-hour drive from Dana Point, at about 7:30 a.m. anxious to begin work. Outside the first floor elevator was a telephone, and I had been instructed to call the A&E director, Tony, on arrival. He took me to the seventh floor and to HR (Human Resources). I spent an hour or so completing the usual paperwork and forms. Then I was taken to get an employee photo ID/building access card. The card was very important since entrance to the seventh floor from the elevators and to the five working suites was gained by swiping the card at each entry door. During the following year, I probably used it fifty times a day.

Then I went to meet the team and find my assigned cubicle.

Within the first hour, I was in a meeting, planning for the initial visit of the Japanese general contractors (GCs) responsible for the construction of Universal Studios Japan (USJ). They would arrive in Hollywood the following week. So much for any casual getting acquainted time and for learning a new job. This was going to be fast.

If I hadn't already been happy about working on a theme park again, my assignment would have convinced me to accept the job. The layout was divided into five areas. I was assigned to Area 3. For the next four-plus years I would be "playing" with the dinosaurs of *Jurassic Park*, the sharks from *JAWS* and all the futuristic gear involved in the *WaterWorld Show*. For a grown-up kid, it sounded like heaven.

Of course, in reality it was very hard work, accomplished with the additional handicap of cultural and language differences.

The GCs were coming in seven days, and I was expected to be all-knowing about my attractions. It was time to "hit the books." By "the books," I mean the Concept Books created about a year earlier, along with the almost completed Concept Refinement Design (CRD—pronounced "Crud") Books.

∗ ∗ ∗ ∗ ∗

A Little History

In 1994, representatives from *Osaka,* Japan and Universal Studios had agreed to build a world-class theme park on fifty-six hectares in the Konohana Ward waterfront area of the city. The *Osaka* Universal Promotion Company (OUPC) was organized to carry out planning and feasibility.

In 1996, OUPC was renamed USJ Co., Ltd. (or "U-S-Jayco") and established as the constructor, owner and operator for the park. This multi-national conglomerate was made up of the major land owners and investors—*Osaka* City, MCA Universal, *Osaka* Gas, *Sumitomo* Metal, *Sumitomo* Corporation, *Nisshin* Steel, Western Japan Railway (*JR* West), Japan Freight Railway and *Hitachi Zosen.* USJ Co. would control expenditures.

By 1997, the preliminary selection of the eighteen attractions and forty-five restaurants and shops had been made. Many of the most popular US attractions, such as *Jurassic Park, E.T., Back to the Future* and *Terminator 2-3D,* were obvious. Others based on adventure films popular in Japan, like *Beetlejuice, JAWS* and *WaterWorld,* were selected. Added to the list were live action shows, including the *Western Stunt Show* and the *Animal Actors Stage.*

The owners asked for a children's area. Universal was fortunate to obtain the international licensing of the characters from the *Peanuts* cartoons to create a section of special appeal to kids. Several additional attractions unique to the park in Japan were added. A large lagoon was planned in the center to accommodate a nighttime show featuring singers and dancers and lots of lights and pyrotechnics.

USJ would contain all the amenities necessary to insure a pleasant experience for the eight million guests expected annually. The date of April 1, 2001 had been selected as opening day for the park.

∗ ∗ ∗ ∗ ∗

The first design phase (Concept Design) had started a year or so before I joined the company. It laid out, in broad terms, the overall arrangement of the park. A series of loose-leaf binders was created to identify each element from the largest ride, attraction, restaurant or store, down to the smallest food stand. During the concept phase, features had been discussed, debated and revised until agreement was reached. The pages in each binder had changed often during that period as ideas were blessed or discarded.

*   *   *   *   *

That first week I read as fast as possible and also prowled "back-of-house" at both the *Jurassic Park* ride and *WaterWorld* show, learning as much as I could about how they worked and what went on behind the scenes. Fortunately, other members of the team (area director, facility design manager, architects and technical engineers) had been planning the presentation for some time and were prepared with renderings, diagrams, drawings and sketches for each attraction.

I also became reacquainted with industry jargon. Theme parks evolved from movies, which evolved from the theater. I had heard most of the terms before but had to get used to using them again. There were no "employees," only "cast members." The areas visible to the public were "on stage." Customers were always called "guests," and the area out of the guest view was "back-of-house." Uniforms worn by cast members were called "costumes." The term "attraction" was used generically for all entertainment venues. But rides were "rides" and shows were still "shows." The studio restaurant "back-of-house" was the "commissary." And the "guest experience" was always our primary concern.

*   *   *   *   *

Week Two

The contingents from the Japanese GCs arrived.

Since I was in Area 3, I would be working with the team from *Takenaka* Corporation. They had come to the US to get a feel for the existing rides and shows as well as to conceptually grasp what an "American" theme park looked and felt like.

The Hollywood creative teams gave presentations. Each one ran from two to four hours and covered an attraction in detail. Early every morning, before the park opened, we walked an attraction. Then, with donuts and coffee in hand, retired to a conference room prepared the night before. Drawings and renderings lined the walls showing the attraction we had just visited. These became the main focal points of our discussions. Led by the area director, each member discussed his or her portion of the project. I gave my limited information on facility needs for utilities and other special requirements I had learned the week before. Boring stuff compared to most of the others.

It was also my first encounter with meetings where everything had to be translated. This made the process twice as long, and we could tell during the question and answer period that the two sides sometimes didn't track together. The translators who came with the GCs had the hardest job keeping up with all the technical terms, acronyms and phrases. Many of these terms were unique to the entertainment industry and unfamiliar to the Japanese.

Our rides in Japan would be using state-of-the-art electronics and animation upgraded from what already existed. The dinosaurs in *Osaka* would move farther and faster than the ones in Hollywood. The *JAWS* ride would have seven sharks, each "swimming" beside and between the ride vehicles. All the characters would have to operate in, around and under water. The challenges were becoming clear.

*   *   *   *   *

During our first week together, we often lunched as a group, and on several occasions chose Japanese restaurants. The first time we used chopsticks (*hashi*), my prowess in eating with the Japanese utensils was praised. "*Jozu na!*" Fortunately, I recognized the term as appreciation for my skill.

I had learned one phrase in Japanese to use in such circumstances, "*Demo mada jozu jarimasen.*" This meant, "But I am not very good yet." It showed the correct level of humility when being praised.

Growing up in Los Angeles, I had enjoyed Asian restaurants and had learned to eat with the implements provided. We had received beautiful chopsticks as a wedding gift, and used them at home. We also used *hashi* when dining with our Asian friends. But I guess the Japanese thought Americans would only know how to eat with western flatware. My abilities would be praised many more times during the next few years. It was one skill I was grateful to have mastered.

*   *   *   *   *

Week Three

The USI team and the GCs flew to Florida to visit the attractions there. So, I found myself in Orlando explaining the *JAWS* ride (which I had never seen) to the contractors, with everything translated through an interpreter. We entered before the park opened and walked "back-of-house" to see how the sharks and other effects actually worked. I made the mistake of standing in the wrong place on the dock when the fire effect was demonstrated. While in no actual danger, standing thirty feet away from a twenty-foot diameter fireball of propane and natural gas had me quickly checking to see if my eyebrows had survived. They had. I played it cool, and my explanation continued as if this were a normal occurrence.

*   *   *   *   *

On our return to California, my boss, known as "Stresh-san" because our Japanese friends couldn't pronounce his multi-syllabic ethnic name, hosted a pool party at his home for the entire group.

Atypically, *Hatenaka-san* had brought his wife and children to California with him. Another guy, *Shimizu-san*, had his wife along. (Japanese business-men almost never included their families in business situations.) The kids enjoyed the water while the adults laughed and gestured trying to understand one another. We were starting to feel more comfortable around each other, despite our lack of verbal communication skill.

On their last night in town, we ate at a local Japanese restaurant. By now we were used to the Japanese custom of eating on low tables while seated on the floor. Many toasts to the success of our endeavor were made, and the first of numerous group photos was taken.

*   *   *   *   *

Our introduction to the *Takenaka* design team was to have a greater impact on the future of the project than any of us realized at the time. For the Japanese, relationships in business are as important—if not more important—than the actual work. Getting acquainted at this stage of the project paid off handsomely later on. But at the time all we knew was there were lots of obsta-cles to overcome, and we would have to work diligently together to solve them. With the basics decided, the work began in earnest.

Culture Clash

Meishi (may-shee)
Japanese name card, as essential to the Japanese as their identi-
ties. Meishi are formally presented at all business meetings.

*   *   *   *   *

Larry

Doing business in the Japanese manner was a learning experience for me along with many of the team members who had not previously worked with them. The process of conducting meetings in the Japanese group style with translators, and adjusting to the Japanese social customs was not easy for most of us—and was never comfortable for some.

Learning to bow was the first challenge. It was necessary to know how low to go in relation to our Japanese counterparts without being too humble (bowing too low) or not respectful enough (not bowing low enough). After a few meetings, the correct length and depth became instinctive, but I had to think about it at first.

Learning to present the *meishi* (name card) in the proscribed manner was another educational experience. In the beginning, just remembering to offer the *meishi* immediately upon first introduction was a challenge. Finding the proper way to hold the card in both hands with the printing facing towards the person being introduced, offering it at the same time they were presenting theirs, bowing correctly, and then studying the card intently all took some repetition before the process became automatic. I also learned not to write on the card and to place it carefully in my business card case. We all began carrying them knowing it would be expected.

I learned how to enter the meeting room in the correct manner. The most senior member of the team would enter first, followed by the rest of the group in descending order of rank. Sitting in the proper spot at the table was the next lesson. We tried to locate a seat facing the door if possible, with the senior members closest to the center of the table. However, the entire team sat on the same side, with the other group opposite. Those closest to the door were assumed to be the least important members. They would be chosen to leave the meeting to make copies or run other errands.

Appearing united as a group and never overtly disagreeing among ourselves was difficult for many of the Americans, but necessary for being taken seriously by our counterparts. Any dissents or differences of opinion had to be tabled until the conclusion of the meeting.

The challenges were greatest when in the US. It was easier to forget the foreign cultural formalities when working on "home turf."

We weren't used to the hierarchical structure found in Japanese organizations. People were accorded respect based on their titles and/or age. This structured approach was expected, and our ignorance of it could cause a rift in relations. More importantly, those assumed to be of lower "rank" were virtually ignored by the Japanese.

Since USI had several female engineers, it was critical we men give them deferential treatment in meetings. We were careful to assure they were not the last to enter the room. We also referred questions to them, even if we were equally capable of answering. By emphasizing their equivalent status with the men, our Japanese counterparts learned to do the same.

In time and with some compromise on both sides, a comfortable working relationship developed.

* * * * *

The design was divided between the Japanese general contractors (GCs) and the Universal Studios International group based in Hollywood (USI). The GCs had design responsibility for the construction of the entire park. The USI team was responsible for the "guest experience." The term "guest experience" covered all aspects of what people would encounter during their visit, including the visual and audio impact of the rides and shows plus their safety and comfort.

Since I was a PE (project engineer), my job was to make sure all the creative designs suggested by other members of the team were constructible and safe. This often meant working out the necessary utilities (power, water, air, steam, etc.) to operate the effects. For instance, one of my early challenges was to figure out how to safely provide enough power and hydraulics to make the fifteen-hundred-pound T-Rex in *Jurassic Park* move thirty feet in three seconds, repeating the action every thirty seconds. And this activity had to run continuously eighteen hours a day, seven days a week.

Our team was optimistic, believing the visit from the Japanese GCs had familiarized them with the look and feel of an American theme park. Then the design drawings began to arrive in Hollywood.

When the US engineers objected to open trench drains along the streets and in and around the buildings on the Japanese drawings, they were told, "That's the way we do it in Japan." After our arrival we noticed most streets did have deep exposed drains running along each side of the very narrow pavement, and nearly every bathroom and kitchen we entered had recessed channels around the walls for drainage as well.

Drawings arrived in Hollywood showing many small air handling (heating and air conditioning) units on the interior ceilings of restaurants, queue lines and other attraction spaces with unsightly ductwork visible to the guests. Our engineering staff reminded the Japanese design team of the requirements for large exterior air conditioners and hidden piping. The reply was, "We don't do it that way in Japan." We later found Japanese buildings—even quite new ones—had only small area air conditioning units. And it was not at all uncommon to look up when inside and see piping and ducting mounted below the ceiling in plain sight.

Our design engineers also attempted to add air conditioning to public restrooms and the cooking areas of restaurants when these were not shown on the drawings. Once again, drawing revisions arrived with the units removed and the explanation, "The Japanese people don't require this." And, once again, our experience in Japan was of restrooms in most train stations uncomfortably hot in the summer and freezing in the winter; and the kitchens in restaurants were often smoky, sultry and stifling.

One of these explanations for basic disagreements in design philosophy— "This is how we do it in Japan." "We don't do it this way in Japan." "The Japanese people don't require this."—fit almost any situation which arose. They became known around the office as the "Japanese mantras."

∗   ∗   ∗   ∗   ∗

The design continued on both sides of the Pacific with different groups from Hollywood making occasional business trips to *Osaka* to meet with the GCs and government officials. Permits and applications were completed and filed.

During the business trips, working relationships continued to be formed and strengthened. Several team members spent their weekends in *Osaka* traveling or looking at neighborhoods for potential future residency. The design phase began to pick up momentum.

Then in May of 1998, the *Mihariban* Citizens' Watchdog Group, the neighbors living near the future site of the theme park on *Sakurajima* (Cherry Blossom Island), filed a lawsuit to stop construction based on the accusation the site was contaminated. Initial studies of the area indicated one corner contained some heavy metals and unexploded WWII ordinance.

USJ Co. immediately called in engineers and environmentalists to complete a detailed assessment of the situation. It was determined the ordinance could be removed fairly quickly. Unfortunately there was a great deal of contaminated soil to be disposed of. Most landfill areas in Japan eventually became new islands. Soil was rarely wasted since there was so little of it to spare. However, because of the contaminants in this particular dirt, finding somewhere to move it proved a major challenge. Eventually, it was relocated on the site itself, placed in plastic-lined concrete containers and buried under the parking lot. The clean soil from that area was moved off-site and deposited in landfills elsewhere.

The eighteen-month cleanup project began in hopes the 2001 opening date could still be met.

And even during the site cleanup, the engineering process continued.

First Trip to Japan

Planes, Trains & Subways

Shinkansen
Japanese high-speed bullet train. There are several categories of trains:

普通	**Local** (*kakueki-teisha* or *futsu-densha*)
快速	**Rapid** (*kaisoku*) (Called the "*Rapi:t*" pronounced "ra-peed" in *Osaka*)
急行	**Express** (*kyuko*)
特急	**Limited Express** (*tokkyu*)

*　　　*　　　*　　　*　　　*

Larry

Plans for the park were progressing to the point where we needed to solidify the infrastructure requirements (water, electrical, sewer systems, etc.) for the entire park. The three general contractors (GCs) paid for a group, consisting of four facility design managers (FDMs), five project engineers (PEs) and two consultants in addition to Tony, the A&E director, to fly to *Osaka* for one week of meetings to fill in missing information and iron out differences. Hooray! It would be my first trip to *Osaka* and first time in Japan.

*　　　*　　　*　　　*　　　*

January 31, 1998

We were booked on a JAL (Japan Airlines) Saturday morning direct flight from LAX to *Kansai* International Airport in *Osaka*, landing late Sunday afternoon February 1st. We took over most of the first class section in the nose of the 747.

Since it was the first (but not the last) of my long flights from L.A. to *Kansai*, I appreciated the superb service and amenities of first class: personal TV screens, wide reclining seats with adjustable leg and head rests (like Barcaloungers in the sky), complementary flight bags with sleep masks, ear plugs, slippers, miniature toothbrushes and paste, hand cream and a gift of a silver spoon in the pattern unique to JAL.

The food in first class was several levels above the usual in-flight fare. We could choose from either Japanese or international cuisines. Being adventurous, I opted for the Japanese-style dinner. But I decided to go for the American breakfast since raw fish, *miso* soup, rice and salad weren't as appealing early in the day. We were served on real china with linen placemats and real silver flatware. Of course, the champagne and other alcoholic beverages were complementary.

We arrived at the *Kansai* International Airport after the eleven-hour flight, checked through immigration and changed some money from dollars to yen at the counter located right at the exit from customs. Then we carted our bags directly to the train station on the second floor, still within the airport, and had our first "*Rapi:t*" (high-speed) train trip from the airport directly to *Namba* station in downtown *Osaka*. The *Rapi:t* train looked like a streamliner from a 1930's science fiction movie. (We called it the "Flash Gordon" train.) It had a sleek, aerodynamic profile and round porthole-type windows on the side. Polarized glass in the portholes allowed the windows to darken using a handle to rotate the inner glass.

Since this train ran on a dedicated track from the airport to *Namba*, the engine pulled the train in one direction and pushed in reverse on the return trip. In each railcar, every row of seats was mounted on a swivel. When the train was cleaned at each end of the run, the rows were rotated 180-degrees so the passengers would always face in the direction of travel.

A smartly suited attendant, in 1950's style Pepto-Bismol pink stewardess uniform (complete with scarf, white gloves and pillbox hat), directed us to our assigned seats and showed us where to stow our luggage. Assigned seats cost an additional ¥500, bringing the fare from ¥1300 to ¥1800 (about $15) but well worth it as we were guaranteed seats in a non-smoking railcar for the thirty-five-minute trip.

The *Namba* station had four levels below ground and two above. In addition to the *Rapi:t*, It was also a major hub for the JR (Japan Rail) trains, the *Nankai* railway and the *Osaka* subway. The lowest two levels contained the subway, the two above were for the trains and the street and second levels contained shops and restaurants.

It was about 7:00 p.m. and the station was still bustling with people headed home from work. It seemed like everyone was running (or at least walking very quickly) somewhere.

Two escalators and one elevator later, we checked in to the *Nankai* South Tower Hotel. The *Nankai* was a five-star hotel located three floors directly above the *Namba* station, very convenient for the weary traveler. We had gone from the plane to the airport to the train to the hotel and still never stepped out-of-doors. We dropped our bags in the rooms and headed out to see the city and get something to eat.

*   *   *   *   *

Since it was February, it was very cold (about 5° C) and had rained just before our arrival. With the narrow streets, heavy crowds, and all the neon signage everywhere, I felt a little like I had stepped into the movie set of "Blade Runner." I was definitely on sensory overload.

Tony, who had made several trips here before and was an old hand at this, directed us to the nearby Hard Rock Café (something familiar) for dinner, followed by a walk around the area before heading back to the hotel.

The main street in *Namba* was a covered shopping street crammed with every kind of shop imaginable. Crowds flocked to this area every evening and stayed until late at night. All kinds of Japanese hung out there: rockers with spiked, dyed hair and assorted piercings; couples dressed to the "nines," slightly drunk "salarymen" in dark suits and loosened ties weaving their way along; young women in very short skirts (yes, short skirts even in the winter) and at least six-inch-high platform shoes. Street vendors and musicians were on every corner, and hawkers bid us enter their stores from many a doorway. To all these add eleven tired but wide-eyed "*gaijin*" (foreigners) and Tony, our guide.

*   *   *   *   *

Monday morning 6:00 am.

Met in the *Nankai* Hotel for the breakfast buffet. (Universal got a special rate.) Then, like baby chicks all in a row, we followed Tony down to the subway for the adventure of negotiating our way to the Universal offices in the *Osaka* World Trade Center.

First, down the escalators and stairs to the lowest level to find the "*Midosuji*" line headed toward "*Honmachi*." This subway line was rumored to be the most

12

crowded in *Osaka*, and I believed it. We were shoehorned in with several hundred people to a car (standing room only). In the subway, there was a definite method (although not publicized) of getting on a busy train. Platforms were marked exactly where the train doors would open. Two lines (one at the edge of each door) were formed. When the train arrived and the doors slid apart, passengers exited in the center of the doorway between the two lines. At the same instant, the lines pushed from each side onto the train.

The secret to getting on board was to "get in a line and go with the flow." After the train was filled to its natural capacity, several designated "pushers" in uniforms and white gloves, added about twenty more people to each car. The entire operation took less than thirty seconds.

Our whole group managed to get on the same train. Once aboard, we were whisked along, listening intently to the recorded conductor's message as it called out the names of the stops (both in Japanese and somewhat understandable English) over the public address speakers. We were all afraid of missing our stop and ending up who knew where. There was a collective sigh of relief when we heard the word "*Honmachi*." Fortunately it was only a few stops. Then up some stairs, down a corridor and down some more stairs to the "*Chuo*" line where we repeated the same get-on-board ritual and picked up the subway to "Cosmo Square." (Ah, an understandable name—in English!) At "Cosmo Square," we changed to the "New Line." (It was called the "New Line" because it was newer than the rest. I wondered what would happen when a newer new line was built.) The "New Line" got us to "Trade Center *Mae*" station. ("*Mae*" means "in front of," so this station was in front of the Trade Center.) From there we had a two-block walk and we finally arrived at the *Osaka* World Trade Center (WTC) where Universal had offices for us on the 28th floor. There we were to hold meetings with the various Japanese contractors who were going to build the park.

*   *   *   *   *

It's necessary to explain the differences in meeting styles between Japan and the United States. In the US, a meeting was generally directed toward making a decision, coming to a consensus, defining a next step. Discussions occurred, and each side participated in give-and-take of opinions and suggestions. Ideas were rejected or accepted and conflicts were "hammered out" during the meeting. Everyone came away with a direction as to how to proceed.

Japanese meetings were somewhat different. In Japan, each group presented their proposal and stance. The positions were discussed, and everyone agreed further "study" was needed. No decision was made at this meeting. Each group then retired to assess their options and a new recommendation was determined within each group. A second meeting was arranged where the new position (usually closer to an agreeable solution) was presented. Sometimes several more "studies" were necessary before a consensus could be reached.

Thus went the first day of meetings: no decisions, just further study. Some of the US contingent were disappointed with the apparent lack of progress, but Tony and others who knew the process said, "Things are going well." And they were.

By the end of the week, much had been accomplished. But the endless meetings were boring, and with the seventeen-hour time difference and jet lag, it was easy to lose concentration and/or "drift off" during negotiations.

*   *   *   *   *

The week went by quickly: Up at 6:00 a.m., hotel breakfast and subway to work. We became accustomed to the route, and within a couple of days, it was no longer necessary for all of us to go together. Schedules were never required, and we soon leaned that the next train headed in the right direction would arrive within three minutes. Meetings were held all morning. At lunchtime we would walk to the Asian Pacific Trade Center (ATC) building directly across the street and accessible by a covered second-floor walkway. The ATC had a wide variety of restaurants and stores and was fun to just wander in and window shop. Those of us who were adventurous tried a different restaurant every day: Thai, Indian, Korean, Italian, French, Japanese, etc. The less adventurous alternated between the Subway sandwich place and Wendy's hamburgers.

Afternoon meetings were held till about 6:00 p.m. Then back on the subway to *Namba*. The group tried out different eateries in the area each night. One of our favorites for very good food was the *Nankai* Grill located adjacent to the *Dotanbori* Bridge. It was a "*teppan*" restaurant like a *Benihana* except at Japanese prices. (Very high.) I was extremely glad we were on expense accounts.

On Friday evening, the Japanese contractors invited us to a *shabu-shabu* restaurant near the WTC to celebrate the successful outcome of our meetings. About fifteen of the Japanese people from the three contractors were there. With the twelve of us from Hollywood, it made a nice mixture of cultures. At the restaurant, everyone sat Japanese-style around low tables, each with a heated pot of boiling water in the center. *Sake* and beer (pronounced "bee-ru") were served. Platters of thin sliced beef strips, vegetables and other (to me unrecognizable) items were brought in. The traditional rice bowl and assortment of dipping sauces (i.e. soy, *wasabi*, fish, etc.) were provided at each place. Everyone selected from a platter using *hashi* (chopsticks) and placed their meat or vegetables in the common pot. It cooked in just a few minutes. The item was then fished from the pot, dipped in a sauce and eaten, all with chopsticks. It was a good test of chopstick proficiency for most of the US team and a chance to learn formal "polite" chopstick etiquette: When moving food from the platter to the group pot and from the pot to the plate, one end (usually the larger) was used. When eating, the sticks were reversed so the normal (smaller end) held the food. Months later when I was dining at a close friend's house in Japan, the host remarked how polite my style was, but mentioned that in an informal setting such as a home with friends, turning of the chopsticks was not necessary.

While our food cooked, the time was spent attempting to converse. Since translators were not available for our dinner, there was a lot of gesturing and stammering for words. But, amazingly, we were able to understand each other. We all had a wonderful time joking and taking group pictures. The combined team of Japanese and Americans who would eventually build the park had begun to bond.

*   *   *   *   *

Our Saturday flight did not leave until evening, so we actually had some free time to see *Osaka*. Several of us decided to get up early and visit *Osaka* Castle. We plotted a route via the subway to get there. I was not feeling very well but decided to go along anyway. The subway station, so busy and crowded during the week, was almost deserted. By the time we reached the castle, I knew I was coming down with something (headache, fever and some nausea). I curled up on a bench while the others climbed the castle. I would have to wait for another day to see it myself.

Fortunately, one member of the group had some aspirin, and I slept during most of the return flight. Leaving at 6:30 p.m. Saturday evening from *Osaka*, we arrived in Los Angeles at 10:00 a.m. Saturday morning, thanks to the International Dateline.

I spent Sunday sick in bed. I think the flight extended the 24-hour bug I had picked up on the trip. But I was well enough to go back to work on Monday, a little better acquainted with doing business Japanese-style.

Hollywood Daze

Sugoi (sue-goy)
Awesome, great, wonderful

*　　　*　　　*　　　*　　　*

Larry

From August 1997 until July of 1998, I worked on the seventh floor of Building 488, located just north of the main soundstages on the Universal Studios Hollywood lot. This gave me a wonderful opportunity to visit the park each day. A quick walk up Tower Street, left turn down Main past the Universal Studio Store, then through a back employee gate, and I would magically appear in the *Jurassic Park* entry area.

After the first week I settled into a lunchtime routine: a quick meal at the studio commissary, then into the park.

First I checked to see if all six torches were operating correctly at the *JP* entry gate. They were pretty fickle on windy days, and we were investigating alternate schemes to keep the flares lit in Japan. Then, shunning the "*Starway Escalator,*" (I needed the exercise.) I would climb the stairs to the upper level and traverse the back-of-house area to *WaterWorld*, usually catching the last few minutes of the noon show. Here I often saw the resetting of equipment and talked to the staff as they prepared for the next performance. A quick, "How did it go today?" usually provided me with information which would be very helpful later at the same attraction in Japan.

Then across the upper level to check progress on the *Terminator 2-3D* show building. Knowing the construction manager, I sometimes got a first-hand update. From this same spot, I had a bird's eye view of the *JP* ride below, checking the operation of the "jeep drop," geysers and other effects.

Finally, I would return to the "*Starway,*" this time taking the stairs halfway down, then exiting back-of-house to follow Firehouse Road past the rear of *JP* to inspect flow and pump status of the waterfalls in the water control room before returning to my office.

My mornings were not neglected either. Arriving at work before park opening gave me about an hour to learn as much as I could about the attractions.

16

This I did at least one day a week the entire time I was in Hollywood. I counted the time there as extremely useful. Besides, for a theme park junkie, it was fun!

*   *   *   *   *

On one of my early morning adventures, an assistant art director, Michael, and I were in the *Jurassic Park* show building near boat lift #2. (Spots where the level of the track went up were called "lifts," and they were numbered from the beginning of the ride to the end for ease of identification.) The vehicles exited this lift into the topmost lagoon, causing a splash that wet the egress path and equipment located there. In Hollywood, a rather unsightly wall had been added as an afterthought to keep the water away from the electrical gear. The lighting was dimmed in the area, and flashing beacons had been placed on the opposite side of the track to draw the guests' eyes away from the soggy area. We were attempting to find a better way to mitigate the water problem.

Looking up, I noticed a boat containing passengers approaching the top of the lift. Normally we'd hear a PA announcement before guests were allowed on the ride, but with all the soundtrack noise (alarm horns, sirens, animal growls, etc.), we must have missed it. Quickly we retreated into the shadows until the boat had passed, then followed behind it (no guest ever looks back) and finally ducked into the safety operator control room next to the start of the eighty-five-foot drop. From that location, an operator monitored each approaching craft (and you thought no one was watching) and could stop the ride if necessary. From behind the booth, we reached the stairs and exited the building.

*   *   *   *   *

Working on a theme park was different from other kinds of projects. As an electrical engineer, I had spent most of my working life in the petrochemical industry. I also had some experience with nuclear and commercial projects, and had a previous taste of theme parks working on an attraction in another park which was never completed. The excitement level was much higher in the entertainment industry. After all, no one cheers when you build an oil refinery in their backyard.

Security was highly important. Industrial spying was always a concern as were safety and corporate integrity. Creative ideas and attractions were kept "under wraps" until a public announcement was made. And insider secrets were never revealed.

I found out about how seriously security was taken in an unusual way. Universal had a great rideshare program. Within a week, I was carpooling with three other riders. Living the farthest away, I would leave Dana Point before 5:00 a.m., pick up the second person in Laguna Niguel, about five miles away, then meet the other two at a shopping center about ten miles further up Interstate 5 toward Los Angeles. From there, we would drive one car the remaining miles to Universal City, arriving before 8:00 a.m., traffic permitting.

Often we would stop by the designer coffee stand in the Universal commissary before heading to our building. "Make mine a mocha cappuccino, extra cream please," was my usual order.

On a desk in our building lobby sat a card-reader. Here we swiped our rideshare cards to get credits redeemable for merchandise from the Universal stores. Carrying a briefcase, coat and coffee cup while passing the card through the reader could become a juggling act.

One morning, after reaching our seventh floor offices, one of the guys remarked, "Darn, I left my briefcase back at the reader and I have an eight o'clock meeting. Could you get it for me?"

"Sure," I volunteered and headed back down in the elevator.

I arrived just as several guards were preparing to cordon off the lobby because of the suspicious unclaimed briefcase located there. My half of the conversation went like this:

> "I've come to pick up that briefcase."..."No, it's not mine."..."Yes, I know who it belongs to."..."No, it probably contains only papers and maybe some fruit for a snack."..."Yes, here's my ID and access card."..."No, I don't believe it's locked."

Several more minutes and repeats of the above conversation were necessary before I was allowed to pick up and open the case (just papers, no fruit). And after promising that the guilty party would not forget again, I was allowed to return to work.

At the time I thought the guards were being a bit paranoid, but I now realize they were just ahead of their time. And doing an excellent job. The case had probably been there less than five minutes.

*   *   *   *   *

During this year we were asked to host yet another Japanese student in our home. Thinking this would be a good cultural refresher in preparation for our upcoming move to Japan, we agreed. So in February of 1998, *Fumiko* arrived.

Our daughter Kim, who lived about six blocks from us, also had a student, *Ikue*, and her neighbor had a third named *Kae*. The three girls, all students at *Nanzan* University in *Nagoya*, spent most of their time together—usually at our house. It was like getting three for the price of one.

One of the customary trips the visiting student groups made was to Universal Studios, Hollywood. Our daughter often volunteered to go along on these ventures as guide and additional driver.

Since I was working there, I thought it might be fun to see if I could show them a "preview" of the park we would be building in Japan. Having personally experienced the zealousness of Universal security, I wanted to make certain I wouldn't violate any rules if I had visitors to the office.

I contacted HR (Human Resources) and asked if guests were allowed. To my surprise, they said it would be fine as long as the group was limited to no more than five, and each of them completed a confidentiality agreement before they arrived. Their names would be given to the building guards who would verify identities before I could escort them to my floor.

So I collected the proper paperwork and had it appropriately completed, signed and submitted. In addition to my daughter and the three students, their Japanese advisor was also very anxious to know about the future park. So she was included in my group of five.

The day arrived. After they spent the morning enjoying the rides and shows in the park, I met the visitors at the back gate and escorted them past the soundstages where several movies and TV shows were in production. They realized the general public was not allowed in this area, and were a bit awestruck.

After checking in with the guards, I was allowed to take them to the seventh floor where they saw many of the sketches, models, "makettes" (scale models of the creatures which would populate the various attractions), color boards and design drawings.

The highlight of their trip was visiting the Model Room where the scale layout of the entire park, handcrafted and meticulously painted, was being prepared for shipment to Japan.

A chorus of "*Sugoi!*" erupted from the group when they realized what they were viewing. This was the first time I had heard the word, and they were quick to translate it for me as "fabulous" or "wonderful" or "awesome." We would also hear it nearly every time a Japanese person saw our apartment in Japan. (But more about that later.)

I was able to give them a "virtual tour" of the areas of the park using the model. They began recognizing some of the attractions they had experienced earlier in the day. There were also some they didn't recognize like *Animation Celebration* and *Movie Magic*. And they were delighted to learn about the entire *Peanuts* area for the kids. Snoopy was the most popular cartoon character in Japan at the time, so having rides featuring him and his friends was something special to look forward to.

"You'll enter past the large globe like you do here in Hollywood," I began. "Immediately in front of you will be the Hollywood area. The streets will be named after famous avenues in Hollywood, California like 'Rodeo Drive' and 'Hollywood Boulevard.' There are lots of stores and restaurants, and the whole area will be covered with a transparent canopy, lighted at night and visible for miles."

"Here's the *E.T ride*," pointed *Fumiko*. "I really liked the bicycles."

"That's right," I replied. "Next is the *Terminator 2-3D* attraction."

"Oh, and there's *Backdraft*!" exclaimed *Ikue*. "It was too hot and the fire scared me."

"I liked *Back to the Future* better," added *Kae*, spotting the ride.

"The Hollywood, New York and San Francisco sets will be used to film movies, commercials and TV shows once construction is completed."

"*Sugoi*," they murmured again.

"Here's my favorite, *Jurassic Park*," said Kim pointing to the large waterfall.

"Mine too," I confessed. "Nearby are Amity Village and *JAWS*. Off to this side is the *WaterWorld* stadium. And next to that is the area with the *Western Stunt Spectacular* and *Animal Actors* shows like the ones you saw this morning.

"I liked the animal show best," said the advisor, and the rest of the group, in typical Japanese fashion, agreed with her.

"The *Peanuts* kids' area is here and will have lots of things for children to do. There will be many other attractions, stores, eating places and fun things to see," I concluded.

"*Sugoi desu!*" they all exclaimed together. ("That's fantastic!") They were looking forward to telling all their friends at home about Universal Studios coming to Japan, and they could hardly wait to see the real thing for themselves.

Into Foreign Territory

Expatriate
*(Also "**expat**") A person who has left their homeland to live or work in a foreign country—usually for a long time*

             *   *   *   *   *

Lorna

Since the plan was to move approximately 150 Universal employees and their families to *Osaka* for periods of up to three years, the planning of the relocation effort began. Two corporate representatives were sent to a seminar on expatriate relocation. One was our friend Pat.

Afterward, she called me. "I'm starting to worry about your move," she said. "The company presenting the event has subsidiaries in foreign countries all over the world, and moves thousands of employees and their families every year. They mentioned some potential pitfalls of the expat experience. I was most concerned when they said they consider Japan the most difficult culture for Americans to adjust to."

"Why is that?" I asked.

"Well, Americans are raised to value independence, while the Japanese revere the group. Also, women are still socially treated as men's possessions. I know you too well to think you'd adjust."

"I have a pretty good feel for the culture," I answered smugly. "I expect to enjoy the change."

"Yes, but you haven't *lived* there," she countered. "Talking about it and visiting are totally different than a move of several years."

"I'm sure we'll be fine. We've moved to other parts of the US and adapted. After all, it's not forever. How hard could it be?"

"We'll be hiring people very shortly to help you with the move and support you while you're away. I've been assured you'll have assistance the whole time."

"That's great."

"Well, the news wasn't all bad. We were also told a few people adjust so well they choose to stay when their foreign service is over."

"I don't see that happening with us," I said firmly. "Our family, friends and home are all here in California. We'll probably be ready to come back when the park is finished. But I am looking forward to a change of pace."

"I'm really concerned because, although Universal sent us to the seminar, they seem to be ignoring the suggestions we brought back," she confided. "The company presenting the event has their home office for Asian operations in *Kobe*, near *Osaka*. They offered to have their relocation specialists handle the moves for Universal. They're already established in the area, have lots of contacts and are well aware of the potential difficulties. But Universal feels the fee for their services is too high, so they declined the offer. I think it may have been a mistake."

"I hope you're wrong," I said, still certain we were in good hands and ready for whatever came our way.

*   *   *   *   *

In March of 1998, a big kick-off meeting was held at one of Los Angeles' finest Japanese restaurants. It was intended as an opportunity for the families who would be moving overseas to become acquainted.

We enjoyed meeting everyone, believing we would become friends in the coming months, but the actual mix of people would change dramatically over time, and most of those we encountered that day never joined us in Japan.

The presentation included photos of available housing, videos about the city of *Osaka* and several speakers with information about living in Japan. We were told classes would be held on cultural differences, how to do business with the Japanese, what to expect in our new homes, etc. Unfortunately, those classes would not begin until several months after Larry and I had already moved to Japan. It was over a year later before the culture coach finally made a trip to *Osaka*. He gave some presentations for us at the jobsite. But by then we had already learned most of the lessons offered the hard way and could probably have taught the classes ourselves.

At the end of the event, we received a large binder with the relocation policy and all the necessary details for our move. There was a lot to digest, but confidence remained high.

*   *   *   *   *

Staffing for our support team began. A coordinator was hired in *Osaka*. She had attended school in the US and her English was excellent. But she was still living at home with her parents, and had never had the responsibility of running a household. She was also young and single and had no idea of the challenges facing a family.

In Hollywood, two equally unseasoned young women were employed. These young ladies were all most sincere in their efforts to assist us in moving and adapting to our new environment. However, dealing with the basic challenges inherent in the process was new to them.

It would be several months after we were already in *Osaka* before the company hired anyone with experience in foreign relocation, and then it wasn't Japanese. Those of us who had been coping with the realities of living in this strange culture were, by then, getting frustrated.

This new director arrived in Japan with promises to improve the situation. In our initial meeting with her, she told us, "I'll be moving to *Osaka* soon to take charge. We realize there are problems with inexperienced Japanese staff, but I'll get a handle on it. Once I'm here permanently, things will be easier."

She returned to Hollywood and remained there for several weeks. Her next trip to *Osaka* was packed with meetings in which she faced many of the same business challenges the rest of us confronted on a daily basis.

I had scheduled an appointment with her just before she was to return to California. I entered her office to find her fuming. "I hate doing business in this country!" she snarled. "I've spent the last several days in non-stop meetings, and haven't accomplished a darn thing. The Japanese won't give me answers to any of my questions, and I feel like the whole trip was wasted!"

I empathized, having experienced the same frustrations. She returned to Hollywood later that day and never relocated.

A few months later, another fellow was hired to head the *Osaka* office, or so we were told. He had been employed in a similar capacity for another company in *Tokyo* for several years. His greatest asset was a working knowledge of the language. He arrived on an orientation trip and was introduced to us. He made one more trip to Japan, then was never seen at the jobsite again. Once more, our hopes were dashed.

Finally, a few months before we began to repatriate, a new gal was sent to *Osaka*. Her primary function was to oversee our exit from the project. She was a real professional and made our return to the US much less painful than our move over. After all the inexperience early on, we treasured her balanced and realistic approach to the process. We all wished she'd been sent much earlier.

*   *   *   *   *

We were chosen to be the first to leave. At the kick-off meeting we were told we would receive at least four months' notice of our departure date, and most people would have between five and six. But in May we were told we would be moving to *Osaka* on July first, and I had yet to visit Japan.

Larry left immediately for a week of business meetings, and I joined him the following week for five days of house hunting. These are observations I made immediately after the first trip, to be shared with the rest of the team.

We are back after a most successful trip to *Osaka*. Larry and I have decided to take the "party house"—the four-bedroom, two-thousand square foot, fifteenth-floor penthouse in *Takarazuka*. It is quite a way from the expat community, but for us, part of the appeal of living there will be getting to know the Japanese people.

I was prepared to like *Osaka*. Opinions of others who have traveled and lived in the area were unanimous: "You'll love it!" Flying into *Kansai* International Airport reminded me of the approach to Honolulu—without the scent of plumeria.

Since we're the first to experience the process, we agreed to see properties in all price ranges, make notes and photograph them so there would be more information available to those following. This made for long and tiring days. In all, we looked at about forty-five different places in four days. Those coming after us will probably only see the fifteen or so fitting their specific needs as expressed on their questionnaires.[2]

Anyone looking for a change from the American lifestyle will find sufficient variety in the *Kansai* area. For people who want more of a sense of the familiar, the *Rokko Island/Kobe* area will provide an environment which feels like home. Every effort has been made to create a comfortable expatriate community there.

Transportation and shopping are convenient. Because people generally don't drive, most necessities can be found within walking distance.

A word about walking: In Southern California, we are so tied to our vehicles we forget the simple—sometimes even

---

[2] The information gathered was used to make suggestions and plans for the house-hunting trip.

meditative—pleasure of walking. In the evenings during our stay, we enjoyed comfortable strolls from the hotel to the Asian Pacific Trade Center (ATC) and *Osaka* World Trade Center (WTC) across the street. Meandering along the wharf side of the ATC and enjoying the lights, waterfalls and fountains is a memory to treasure. It is also easy to catch the train to the *Namba* station and enjoy the bustle of people in the city.

The Japanese sense of the aesthetic was apparent to me during the week. Despite having houses pushed tightly against each other, in nearly every block one can find unexpected and charming reminders of grace and beauty: the glimpse of a perfect small flowerbed, an exquisitely designed gate or tiny window, a two-foot by two-foot space turned into a serene rock garden, a perfectly trimmed tree or a miniature waterfall or fountain.

Even the rivers flowing through communities have been terraced to form ledges where water drops into pools below. Riverbanks are lined with paths shaded by trees. During the summer, families picnic under the leaves. In the early mornings, joggers enjoy exercising there. After school, children make their way home in the shelter of the trees. And in the evenings, young people stroll along the pathways.

Those who are intimidated by the language, particularly written, can put their fears to rest. Much of the signage in the cities is in Japanese and English. Universally recognized symbols are used everywhere. Many people here speak a smattering of English, and teenagers sometimes enjoy practicing their skills with you. In fact, they seem somewhat disappointed if foreigners try to converse in Japanese.

There is no need to be concerned about the house hunting process either. The relocation team has chosen realtors specializing in moving foreigners to the area and interpreters who are fluent. A couple of our translators were American-born émigrés to Japan.

Despite warnings to expect small Japanese rooms, we were pleasantly surprised to find many of the properties spacious enough to accommodate our queen-size bed and larger

American-style furniture. A couple of our Japanese exchange students had also told us, "There are no dishwashers in Japan." That myth was dispelled. While most places we saw didn't have them, they can be found in some western-style apartments and houses. This was a priority for me and may be for you as well.

For those coming with families, we were shown some great places close to bus stops for the international schools. I can imagine no better environment for youngsters. We saw them riding unaccompanied on busses and trains with ease and in safety. This generation of Japanese parents is very indulgent with their progeny. So, unlike our expectation of silent, serious and well-behaved children, this generation of kids is much more like ours—for better or worse!

A few tips for those coming after us:

1. The flights are long, so take off your shoes and put on socks or slippers to be more comfortable.

2. Watch the movies, bring a good book or try to sleep. The time will pass faster.

3. Bring slip-on shoes! When looking at houses, it's important to always remove your shoes when you enter. It's much easier with slip-ons.

4. Bring your sense of adventure and fun. The people in the *Osaka* relocation office are delightful and want your trip to be successful.

5. Enjoy *Osaka*!

*   *   *   *   *

So, there we were, dumb and happy.

I gave notice at work for the end of June, anticipating July 1st relocation. Unfortunately, Universal didn't get Larry's work visa in time, so we were delayed a month. Our Dana Point house was rented and our furniture packed and on the ship to Japan, so we moved to temporary housing for the additional month we remained in California.

So it was that, on August 1, 1998, we finally boarded the plane for *Osaka*. Due to the International Dateline, we arrived on August 2, excited about starting out on our great adventure—despite Pat's concerns.

The Honeymoon Begins

Gaijin (guy-gin or guy-jean)
Japanese word meaning "foreigner". (Literally: someone from another country) Sometimes used derogatorily.

* * * * *

Lorna

These are observations I made early in our stay:

> We have now been here for ten days and this is my first chance to record my impressions of the country.
>
> The people, on the whole, are extremely friendly and helpful—probably far more so than in the US—while at the same time retaining a formality and dignity Americans lost a century ago.
>
> There have been some frustrations, like driving the first time on narrow Japanese roads on the left-hand side with a right-hand drive car, without being able to read many of the signs, in a rainstorm trying to follow a road map written in Japanese. What should have been about an hour's drive from the hotel to our place in *Takarazuka* took nearly three hours.
>
> The washer requires about two hours to complete one tiny load, and the dryer takes even longer. They are considered the best available. I have taken to calling them "the Evil Ones."
>
> The county is beautiful. And we are fortunate to have one of the greatest views in all Japan. Standing on our balcony in the morning, smelling the fresh air, looking out over the valley to *Osaka Bay* and seeing the green hills is a balm for the soul. And the same view at night with all the lights twinkling below is a joy to the senses.
>
> In *Takarazuka*, we are something of an oddity. There are few foreigners (*gaijin*) in this area. Although yesterday we spotted two others within one hour. We were all stared at.

Some peculiarities have made us chuckle. In the evening during rush hour, there are police at every major intersection in their uniforms—including the obligatory white gloves—directing traffic. The taxi drivers also wear white gloves. Larry is talking about getting himself a pair to wear while driving in order to "blend in." I told him it wasn't going to help. We are never going to "blend in." [*He eventually got a pair of his own. He didn't blend in.*]

All taxis and some private cars have white lace seat covers. The car Larry is currently driving has them too.

There seem to be many anomalies, contradictions and quirks. For example, the Japanese are enamored of everything technical, but there are still many places in the country which have deliberately not been automated.

All tollbooths are still manned, and drivers have to stop every few kilometers to pay the toll. I asked why they didn't have transponders like we do and was told, "Why, if we did that, the toll takers would be out of jobs." This is also why there are police on every corner during rush hour directing traffic.

And we were told this is the reason there are only a couple of self-service gas stations in Japan. Most have at least three people working: one to pump the fuel, one to wash the windows and check the tires, and a third to assist vehicles exiting the station. When cars are ready to leave, this person stands in the street and blocks oncoming traffic so there is room to return to the flow.

We've adopted a term for some things we've encountered: "Inconvenient by Design." For instance, there are seven faucets in our penthouse, and no two of them work alike. There are two hi-tech toilets, complete with heaters, washers and dryers, yet each of the controls is unique, and they flush differently. One of them even has a remote control that looks like the one for a TV. (Don't ask.) This means we have to concentrate on how to turn the water on and off each time, and remember which toilet we're using and how to flush it. As I told Mr. K, "I think this is more technology than I really need in my life."

Mr. K is the furniture supplier who provided our refrigerator, air conditioners, light fixtures and drapes. "K-san" came over to install the TV dish and also explained how to use the toilets and other equipment with Japanese controls—and Japanese manuals.

✶   ✶   ✶   ✶   ✶

Restaurants

The signs might have looked the same as eateries in the US, but the menus were often very different. In one, the club sandwich consisted of two slices of thin crust-less bread with undercooked bacon, fried egg, lettuce and tomato. It was served with French fries—about six of them.

There was another chain with a name we remembered from Hawaii. Inside, it seemed much more familiar. Their club sandwich was bacon, turkey (I thought)[3], lettuce and tomato. Larry ordered pasta with shrimp and said it was good. And they served pancakes all day.

Eating out was something of a challenge at first. Unless we went to a restaurant chain with English menus, I liked having someone with us who could read Japanese. Things weren't always what they appeared to be, even with picture menus and "plastic food" in the windows.

Bakeries

There were great French bakeries and lots of them. All the major train stations had several, and they could also be found on nearly every block in the cities. Our friend Kay who grew up in the area had told us how good they were before we arrived, and she knew what she was talking about.

Cleanliness

The day the movers were to deliver our furniture, I was standing on the balcony enjoying the view. At 9:00 a.m., two ladies in tan pants, pink smocks and head scarves came out of the building below and began cleaning the driveway and entrance. Further down the hill, some of the shopkeepers were sweeping their front walks preparing to open. I heard the building maintenance people

---

[3] We later discovered that luncheon meat could be anything—including kangaroo. I was happy when I learned to read enough Japanese to tell the difference.

in the mornings working in the hallway in front of our unit. The image of cleanliness which I had associated with Japan certainly seemed accurate.

Trash

Waste removal was very complicated.

Newspapers had to be folded in a proscribed manner, bundled, tied and placed in a specified location in the parking structure. Cardboard boxes were broken down, tied and stored with the newspapers. These were collected twice a month on specific days.

Kitchen garbage (no disposals there) as well as regular trash was tied securely in plastic bags and placed in communal bins in the trash storage area to be hauled away three times a week—Monday, Wednesday and Friday.

Plastic bottles and similar containers had to be washed and bagged and deposited in different bins than the regular trash to be picked up at the same time. Metal cans and glass bottles were removed twice a month from the regular area, but on different days than the trash, newspapers and cardboard.

Other items (broken dishes, toys, etc.) were picked up once a month, and large items (furniture, etc.) were collected on specific dates three times a year.

The trash bins were only open between midnight and 8:00 a.m. on pickup days.

Keeping track of the schedule was so challenging I had to color code our calendar.

∗   ∗   ∗   ∗   ∗

A couple of weeks after our arrival, two of our relocation coordinators came for a visit along with their Japanese friend. He had taken Larry's ten-foot long surfboard from the airport to his home when we arrived because he owned a large enough vehicle to transport it. He only stayed long enough to take a quick look at the place and deliver the board. Larry had to haul it up the fifteen flights of stairs since it was too long for the elevator.

All our guests were impressed by the apartment. There were exclamations of, "*Sugoi!*" (Wonderful!) We eventually became accustomed to hearing it whenever a Japanese person saw the view for the first time.

We managed pretty well early on. All except for the can opener which didn't seem to like the voltage drop. We added a manual opener to our shopping list.

∗   ∗   ∗   ∗   ∗

Shortly after he was hired, Larry had talked to the Architecture and Engineering (A&E) director, Tony, to see if there was anything I could contribute to the project while in Japan. Since we had decided we would be moving overseas together, it required giving up my job in California. To my delight, Tony said there was already an open position on the organization chart for a document control supervisor in the *Osaka* office to be responsible for three other employees. This slot was for a locally-hired person, which meant the salary would be paid in yen with Japanese benefits, and I would have to get a work visa after we were established in Japan. (Larry continued to be paid in American dollars through Universal Studios in California and arrived with his work visa on his passport.)

Tony said he was delighted to be getting my experience and agreed it was a "done deal" and advantage for all concerned. At that point, I just had to move to Japan to be formally hired.

However, Tony left USJ almost immediately after we arrived, and my employment process started anew. In September I interviewed twice more and expected to be working on the project with Larry beginning in October. I missed the discipline of a job, but the extra time allowed me to get the apartment settled and learn about our new neighborhood.

*   *   *   *   *

During those early days, we often thought about people who left Europe and sailed for America or those who headed west in covered wagons. They didn't have the telephone, fax, email or any of the other technology which made it easy for us to conduct business and stay in touch with our families and friends half the world away. And we were grateful to be living in our own time.

We also remembered friends who had served in Africa with the Peace Corps.

Ruth and Dave, who spent several years in Liberia and Kenya, spoke often of the difficulties they experienced adjusting to the culture early in their stay.

Jasmine and Malcolm went to Lesotho for five years after they had already retired and were in their 60s. During most of their service, they lived in the villages with the natives.

Whenever we encountered problems or frustrations, we would remember their stories and laugh at the extreme contrast with our fifteenth-floor luxury penthouse apartment with the fabulous view. It helped keep our situation in perspective. As we faced each new challenge, one or the other of us would invariably say, "Well, it's not a mud hut in Africa." And we would laugh.

We were beginning to adjust to our new way of life…and it was certainly <u>not</u> a mud hut in Africa!

Chores and Challenges

Inkan (ing-kahn)/Hanko (hahn-ko)
Personal seal or stamp bearing the surname which served the same purpose as a signature on official documents. They were always used with red ink.

*   *   *   *   *

Lorna

Being the initial family to relocate, we anticipated some hiccups in the process. We thought perhaps one reason we were selected to be first was because we had some resources already in the country. During the years prior to our move to Japan, we had hosted several Japanese students in our home. Two of them lived in the *Osaka* area. We hoped we could turn to our "kids" if the Universal team wasn't available.

In addition, my close friend, Kay, who was born and raised in *Kobe,* had sent me a long, detailed letter recommending where to live and shop, how to get around and even suggesting an English-speaking church for us to attend. So we thought we were well prepared. Of course, we were wrong.

*   *   *   *   *

One of the first orders of business when we arrived was registering with the city government. We were not aware until we actually got there that *Takarazuka*, our new home, was quite a large place. It boasted the *Takarazuka Revue*—the internationally known all-female theatre troupe. (They can be seen as the theatrical performers in the movie *Sayonara*.) The city had evolved from a group of natural hot springs and was also a resort area.

One of our Japanese daughters, *Yuka*, volunteered to accompany us to the city hall to register. She met us at our hotel and led the way through crowded stations, on and off several trains, and finally on a very long hike through winding streets until we reached our destination. It was a good thing she was with us the first time as I doubt we could have found it on our own. And it was HOT! And HUMID! I never did adjust to the sauna conditions of the Japanese summers.

As a welcome gift, *Yuka* gave us an *inkan* with our last name in Japanese. It was a thoughtful and most practical present since it was impossible to conduct any business in Japan without one. The *inkan* or *hanko* took the place of a signature, which was not recognized.

In addition to identifying ourselves and our place of residence to the city, we had to register the *inkan* (in Larry's name only) as his "official" signature. We purchased several certificates for the *inkan* which we would need for other legal transactions. These documents were only good for ninety days, so if we required more beyond that time, the whole process would have to be repeated.

The strange part of using the *inkan* to us was, if we'd had a common Japanese name, we could have gone to the local stationery store and bought a ready-made one off the rack. In our case, however, a custom one was required. Of course, the specialized ones for English names, written in Japanese *katakana*[4] characters, were considerably more expensive than the "generic" Japanese ones in *kanji*.

When we returned to the office after this excursion, Larry told the coordinator, "Everyone is going to need an *inkan* as soon as they arrive so they can complete their registrations."

"Well, the English ones in *katakana* are pretty expensive, and we don't have that budgeted. Maybe they can get their own like you did," she suggested.

"The rest of the people coming here won't know they need one until they arrive. By that time, it will already be too late," Larry answered. "Besides, where would they get them in California?"

"Oh, I hadn't thought about that. I guess we'll have to take care of it for them," she conceded.

We already had an *inkan*, so the company was saved the cost of purchasing another for Larry.

In a country which didn't use checks, salaries were paid either by making a deposit directly into a bank account, or putting cash in an envelope and handing it to the employee. For cash payments, an *"office lady"* (or *"OL"* as they are known) collected each employee's *inkan* in a box, then took them all to the bank and "signed" for every person's pay envelope. Forgery didn't seem to be much of an issue in Japan.

---

[4] There are three written Japanese languages in addition to *Romanji*, or our alphabet. *Kanji* are the Chinese characters, *hiragana* is the phonetic alphabet for Japanese words and *katakana* is the phonetic alphabet used for foreign words.

When I was hired locally, I was told my money would be deposited directly. But we discovered it could only be transferred to an account in my name. When we inquired about a joint account, we were told, "We don't have joint accounts in Japan." I would also need my own *inkan*. I decided to go against the rules and order mine in *hiragana*, a different Japanese written language. A rebellious American to the last!

*   *   *   *   *

After going to the city, we had to register with the equivalent of our county or prefecture, *Hyogo-ken*.

Allowing enough time to get lost once or twice, we managed to find our way on the train to the offices in *Kobe*. There we joined a translator and the area development director, Berj, and his family who had just arrived. They were as excited about the move to Japan and building the park as we were.

Our task that day was to begin the process of getting our official alien registration ID cards. Once again we were asked the purpose of our stay, how long we'd remain and the location of our residence while in the country.

Our official identification would be sent within a few days. The translator told us, "You must carry your alien cards with you at all times. If you are stopped for any reason without them, you could be deported immediately."

A consular official reinforced this warning. "Be very conscientious about observing all the immigration laws in Japan because they are strictly enforced. Any infraction could be cause to expel you, and we have very little influence over those decisions."

*   *   *   *   *

One last registration with the local police was required. There were "police boxes" or "*koban*" located every few blocks. We learned to distinguish these buildings by the red lights over the doors and the gold star logos. They were manned by neatly-uniformed and white-gloved officers who were aware of every person in the area and their activities. This information came to them, in part, through the police registration.

Larry went to the city's main station and completed the required forms. It took several officers' combined limited English skill to assist Larry in filling in the personal information, including the number of people residing in his household and all our daily routines.

On several occasions during our stay we entertained guests for extended periods. Each time, after the first couple of days, a polite officer would knock on our door to find out who they were and what they were doing there. It was a bit of a challenge on both sides since the local constabulary did not speak English, and our guests did not speak Japanese. But there was an official document with blank spaces, and our friends were able to figure out where to write their names, home addresses and dates of departure.

A few days after our visitors left, the officer would again arrive at our door, clipboard and written information in hand, to make sure they were gone as scheduled.

*   *   *   *   *

Following all the registrations, we began dealing with the daily challenges of adjusting to our new lives. Some of the issues we encountered were:

Internet Access and Email

Although it was a considerable extra expense, the relocation team recommended we have an ISDN[5] high speed line installed because, we were told, our computer would not connect to the Internet without it. The ISDN and Japanese software were installed. However our computer wouldn't recognize the line or the foreign program. Two different consultants tried and failed to get the system to work.

In desperation, we bypassed the special line entirely and used the computer's built-in modem. We were then able to contact one bank, but were still unable to reach an Internet provider. So we had neither email nor connection to any of our other US banking institutions for about 6 weeks. Finally a couple more "experts" arrived and resolved the problem without the use of the ISDN line. It was just one of several ultimately unnecessary expenses we incurred.

Bank Accounts

Before relocating, we were told we could establish both our US and Japanese accounts with the same bank before we left the US. But, although they shared the same name, the Japanese institution was actually a separate company and accounts had to be opened locally.

---

[5] Integrated Services Digital Network

This bank had over a hundred locations in Japan. However, only three of them were in our prefecture, all more than an hour away from either our home or office. Business hours were between 9:00 and 12:00 in the morning and 1:00 and 3:00 in the afternoon, on weekdays only. Larry was finally able to take enough time away from the office to open a Japanese account in addition to our US one. We eventually opened three more accounts: two with one local bank for direct deposits and bill paying—Larry and I each had separate ones—and an account with a different local bank to be used only by the company for paying our Japanese taxes.

Cars

Before our move, we had made it clear we would require a personal vehicle; but when we arrived in *Osaka*, a company transportation policy hadn't been written. Larry met with representatives of three different manufacturers before discovering we were prohibited by law from making a purchase, leasing or acquiring insurance in the country without a written guarantee from Universal. By the time the car policy was completed the following April, the period remaining on our stay was reduced sufficiently that leasing was no longer an option.

Japanese Language Lessons

The move agreement stated the company would provide each of us with three hours of Japanese language lessons per week. However, no arrangements were made for an instructor.

In October, a new project engineer arrived and decided to hire his own teacher and bill the company for her services. At that point, the rest of us were given permission to do the same. We were able to hire the USI lead translator, *Maki*. During our stay in Japan she became like another daughter to us, and was a fine teacher as well. The official instructor for the group was not secured until March of 1999.

Statements from Universal

For our first 5 months in Japan, not one of the payroll detail sheets was on time or accurate. There were huge discrepancies from month to month, and it was very difficult to budget. The accounting department at Universal seemed overwhelmed by all the foreign tax implications, cost of living and housing allowances and other items involved. It took until well into 1999 before we began receiving the correct figures within a reasonable timeframe.

Out of Sight…

Thirty-three families were originally scheduled to relocate by the end of September 1998, but only eight had arrived by the end of December of that year. With so few of us in Japan and so many in Hollywood, our needs were not a priority for the corporate office. But perhaps our group of early arrivals bonded well because of our common challenges.

TBD-san

Obon ($\bar{O}$h-bon)
A traditional Buddhist festival which takes place throughout
Japan in mid-August

                 *   *   *   *   *

Larry
Week One:

My first week in the office at the *Osaka* World Trade Center was spent in meetings like those on my first trip, only now I was there permanently (at least for a couple of years). When not in meetings, I was setting up a cubicle, getting office keys, a building access card and new *meshi* (business cards, a necessity in Japan). I was now officially part of *Universal Studios Recreation, Japan Supervision Inc.,* although everyone still referred to us as USI (Universal Studios International). The cards, complete with the *Osaka* WTC address, were quick to arrive.

Unfortunately my computer was not. I spent most of the first week borrowing others' linked to the network in California. My own machine from Hollywood was shipped to arrive when I did, but it wasn't there. I phoned the project assistant, Christiane, in Hollywood. "Do you remember when my PC was packed before I left?"

"Sure," she said. "I sent it to the mailroom."

"Well, it isn't here."

"It isn't?"

"No. Could you track the shipment?

"You know, I never got the tracking number. I'll do my best to find it for you." I was confident the errant computer would be located quickly.

The next day she called. "I've asked everyone, and no one has seen the box. The people who picked it up have no records. And there is nothing to indicate it ever made it to the mailroom. But I'll keep checking."

"Thanks." I knew she wouldn't relent, but I really needed my own PC with my own records on it.

A day later the phone rang. "Guess what," Christiane started. "I finally found your computer under a desk in a vacant cubicle here in Hollywood. I called to have it picked up and followed it to make sure it was sent this time."

I thanked her, my faith in her confirmed.

But when the computer finally arrived, I discovered another foul-up. It seemed my Hollywood email account had been closed, wiping out my correspondence and files. All my project history was gone. I had stored the information there at the company's direction so I wouldn't have to carry it halfway around the world in hard copy. This resulted in several conference calls with Hollywood to establish a procedure so others didn't suffer the same fate.

*   *   *   *   *

I found the Japanese office layout at the *Osaka* WTC different from what I had expected. In most large US high-rise buildings, managers and directors occupy the window offices around the periphery of the building, with the coveted corner ones reserved for senior management. Restrooms, break rooms and utilities would be relegated to the central core and huddled somewhere near the elevators.

In the Japanese portions of the *Osaka* WTC, the reverse was true. The managers occupied desks in the center of large "bullpens" surrounded by their subordinates. Those with highest rank sat the closest to the bosses, with those of lesser status farther away. Workers who were not performing were relegated to the desks closest to the windows. These people were given little responsibility in hopes they would get bored and quit. In fact, having a window spot was shameful, and those who were positioned in this way were often forced out. They were called *Madogiwa Zoku* meaning "bored men by the windows" or "Window Managers."

Our area was a little more American with cubicles filling the "bullpen" areas. Our managers had actual offices located toward the outside of the large suites. However, no one had a corner office.

The best views to be had on the 28th floor were from the men's and women's restrooms located at each corner of the building. While standing at a urinal, I could gaze at a panoramic view of the city of *Osaka* spread before me. However, I was discouraged from lingering too long as, at any moment, one of several elderly Japanese cleaning ladies, each about four feet tall and equipped with bucket, rags, brush, work apron and headscarf, would enter to scrub the fixture just vacated. The first time it happened was a shock, but after several occurrences, I accepted it as the norm. I secretly wondered if they had a closed-circuit camera to know when cleaning was necessary, or if they just liked to arrive unannounced. But, I must admit, those were the cleanest restrooms I saw in all Japan.

∗   ∗   ∗   ∗   ∗

Week Two:

My second week was *Obon* week. Before we relocated, we were told we would be observing the Japanese holidays. But *Obon* was not listed on the official schedule from Universal, so I had to work.

The GCs and USJ Co. were off celebrating. Japanese businesses usually allowed their employees three or four days for this holiday during which the Japanese paid their respects to their ancestors. Families returned to their towns of origin to visit the family grave site. There were no Japanese in the office.

The Hollywood people on business trips stayed in California. After all, they would have had no one to meet with. And Lorna hadn't officially started yet.

The only person in the *Osaka* office was me.

I arrived each morning about 7:00 a.m. local time (4:00 p.m. in California), unlocked the door, turned on the lights and made phone calls to Hollywood before everyone went home. After 9:00 a.m., it was very quiet. Noon was a welcome break for lunch with Lorna at one of the restaurants at the ATC (Asian Pacific Trade Center).

At the end of the day, I turned off the lights, locked the door and walked back to our hotel. It did give me much-needed time to unpack my office boxes, find furniture for my cubicle, and fill the two 5-drawer file cabinets with records shipped prior to my arrival.

In addition, I spent about two days attempting to program my phone using instructions written in Japanese and listening to the automated responses from the phone—also in Japanese. Unfortunately, the translators were also away for the holiday. I continued to try to locate other people's copies of my lost email. During *Obon* week, I saw not one other person in our offices. Even the cleaning ladies were gone.

By the following year, several directors had relocated. When they discovered the disparity between the official holiday schedule and the actual local work schedule, they insisted we be allowed time off whenever the Japanese were not working. Therefore, we celebrated the next two *Obon* weeks along with our coworkers. In fact, in our last year in Japan this holiday was significant for us. But the first year was lonely.

*   *   *   *   *

Week Three:

USJ Co. and the GCs returned, fresh from their time away. The place was again bustling with people, and there were meetings, meetings, and more meetings.

Because I was the only relocated expat in *Osaka* for the first month, I attended almost all of them for every area, substituting for others who would arrive later. There were several people making business trips at the time, but they were in the office one week and gone the next.

When I first arrived in Japan, much information was still to be confirmed, and many items were marked "TBD" (**To Be Determined**). As information became available, "TBD" would be replaced with the data.

This led directly to my nickname.

Often the answers to questions were outside my scope of responsibility. I couldn't respond for others who were still in Hollywood without their knowledge or consent. It happened so often, I became "TBD-san" in meetings with the GCs. They used "TBD" as if it were my name, and attached "san" to it since it is the honorific equivalent of "Mr." or "Mrs." in English.

When I didn't have a ready answer to a question, the GC would mark "TBD" next to the item. Following the meeting, I would email or phone the US with the issues for which responses were required. When I received the answers, I would relay the information to the GCs. Since getting a definitive reply sometimes took days, or even weeks, "TBD" often remained on the notes and drawings for a long time.

I didn't know quite how to interpret the new nickname, so I mentioned it to the head translation contractor with whom I had worked in Hollywood. He was born in Japan, but lived in the US for twenty years.

"It's good," he explained. "It means the GCs are relaxed enough to joke with you. Japanese rarely use first names, and they wouldn't label you something even less formal if the situation were serious or if they didn't like or trust you. They only give nicknames to those they're comfortable with."

I felt better after that, and in time came to enjoy my new identity.

Eventually information was filled in, the appropriate people arrived in Japan and my name returned to "Rarry-san" (or "Rally-san").

Typhoons

Typhoon (tye-hoon)
A violent tropical storm originating in the western Pacific Ocean

*　　*　　*　　*　　*

Lorna

We grew up in California and endured earthquakes, electrical storms, heavy rains and a few flash floods. We had also lived in Illinois and Denver and experienced tornadoes. And on a memorable cruise, we felt the edge of a hurricane. But during our stay in Japan we survived not one, not two, but three typhoons.

*　　*　　*　　*　　*

September 22, 1998—Typhoon

About 8:30 in the morning Larry called me at home from work to warn me they had been able to tell by the news reports on the radio that a typhoon was headed our way. The words "typhoon" and "*Osaka*" were understandable—even in Japanese.

About 9:00 our Japanese daughter *Yuka* called to make sure I had heard about the storm. I assured her I had, but thanked her for her concern and asked what I should do. She said, "Just close everything up and wait it out." This was where tornado training came in handy.

I began watching the Japanese news programs to see what was happening. Normally we got the Asian weather forecast in English on CNN International, but not that day. CNN had preempted all its programming to show the Clinton tapes.

I was able to see satellite pictures on the Japanese news, and it looked as though the eye of the storm might pass right over our area. I also learned how to read "*Osaka*" in Japanese. Larry had a Japanese map of *Osaka* City which had the *kanji* (Chinese characters) for "*Osaka*" on the front. I compared it with the names listed on the news charts, and found I could recognize it. The adventure became a learning experience.

The news reports indicated a typhoon watch would be in effect for *Osaka* and *Hyogo-ken* (our prefecture) from noon until midnight. There were light winds and some small showers during the morning, but just before noon, the sky turned darker and the rain really started pouring down. Then the wind came up. It was supposed to have been blowing between thirty and fifty knots and sounded like it, roaring around the building.

I shot some videotape during the storm. Unfortunately, every time I turned on the camera, the storm died down. Maybe it was camera shy. I didn't even try to film during the worst of the deluge. The wind was blasting the rain into the windows so hard it sounded like hail, and water blew up under our front door. The door was well insulated but was no match for the gale.

As it was, *Kyushu*, the island to the south of us, took the worst beating where the storm came ashore. Later pictures showed roofs ripped off houses and lots of trees and signs down. Waves were five meters (fifteen feet) and higher. But they were even too rough for Larry to want to surf.

He called from work about 12:30 p.m. and said they were planning on leaving soon as the building was really beginning to sway. (Actually, he said they were getting seasick.) By then, both airports (*Osaka* International and *Kansai*) and some train stations were closed. This meant Larry had to drive two guys home, then over the mountain to get back to *Takarazuka*. He normally picked them up and dropped them off at a station about halfway between our apartment and the office.

All the elevated highways and bridges were closed. Larry normally took one of the big suspension bridges for the first few kilometers. It was more direct and faster than the circuitous surface route. However, he had no choice. He called me back about 2:30 to say they were still on their way to *Ashiya*. They had been slowed by downed tree limbs and other debris on the road as well as the traffic.

Once they reached *Ashiya*, he dropped each of the others at their houses. By this time, it was near 4:00 p.m. The skies had cleared a bit, so he took the shorter route over the mountain rather than the longer one around the bottom. He arrived home just before 5:00.

During the height of the storm, I watched part of our big wind chime go flying out over the railing of the balcony. We each kept a pair of rubber sandals out there. They flew away one-by-one. I also thought I saw one of our plastic chairs blow away, but they were all accounted for. So it must have been something else zooming by the window.

*   *   *   *   *

October 18, 1998—Typhoon, the Sequel

We survived typhoon Zeb, as it was called on CNN. This one traveled directly over us. From all the noise it made, we would have guessed as much.

When we went to bed the night before, the sky was so crystal clear the lights below us seemed to shimmer and sparkle. We really thought the storm was dying down.

The weather reports were quite accurate, though. The forecast was for the storm to hit at midnight. We woke about that time with the wind howling around the building.

I was especially nervous as I slept about three feet from the twelve-foot high, fifteen-foot long glass windows and doors going out onto our bedroom balcony. When I looked out at the balcony, the heavy divider separating our portion from that of our next-door neighbors seemed to be flexing about five inches in either direction. The divider consisted of a heavy metal frame with a Masonite panel in the center. It was bolted to the building. I could just imagine the whole thing coming loose and crashing through a window. I wasn't about to be lying there if anything happened.

At first we went into the center of the apartment in the laundry room next to the center atrium.[6] Larry'd had the foresight to bring all the patio furniture into that area earlier in the day. Everything there was just fine. Thank goodness we had the enclosed space.

Larry figured out our guestroom was, in fact, nearly in the center of the building. We huddled together for the next hour and a half on the guest bed. The wind made such a racket, at one time it sounded like a huge catfight. There were lots of bangs and thumps and bumps and crashes. We did not venture forth to investigate. Neither did we sleep.

About 1:45 a.m. the howling began to die down somewhat and we decided to go back to bed. First, however, we did a quick check to evaluate the damage.

---

[6] Our apartment had a glassed-in open air space in the very center we called the "atrium." It was accessed by two doors off the hallway.

As I had feared, the panel had come out of the frame and shattered all over the bedroom balcony. Fortunately, the metal frame held, and no glass was broken. The screen on the sliding door of the living room balcony was blown completely off. Other than those items, we had no damage. All the windows were intact and the building stayed solid. I was very happy we didn't live in old-style Japanese housing (light wood and paper construction) or it would surely have blown down.

The story of the Three Little Pigs had a whole new meaning.

*   *   *   *   *

September 23, 1999—The Rescue

September fifteenth was a national holiday—*Respect for the Aged Day*. Larry had decided to go to *Wakayama* early in the morning to go surfing. I stayed home to await the repairmen who were scheduled to come and fix the washer. Repairmen in Japan actually showed up exactly when they were scheduled. Just before they came, Larry called to say he was on his way back to *Takarazuka*. It was raining.

The men arrived about 9:30. As they removed their shoes, I heard the word "typhoon." Apparently we were about to be hit with the edge of another storm—and Larry was, once again, out driving in it. It had been overcast and drizzling most of the morning, but the wind came up in earnest, and the rain started pounding sideways against the windows. Larry called again from the loop road in *Osaka* to say traffic was barely moving.

The winds increased. The rain increased. The verdict came in on the washer: The motor had died. One of the repairmen made a couple of trips down to his truck for parts amid the tumult. And herein lies a contrast to the repair scenario in the US—they came prepared with all the required parts. And they were willing to go to the truck—in the midst of a typhoon—to get them.

I kept checking the balcony, but everything seemed to be holding up okay.

Larry arrived shortly before noon, very tired and very wet, another adventure on the roads successfully completed.

The washer was tested while all of us—Larry, both repairmen and I—watched, nodded, approved and declared it fit for use again. This meant it was back to taking two hours to do a load of clothes, but at least the water drained out at the end of the process.

After the repairmen left, we discovered one patio table, which had been left out on the balcony, had made an escape. It ended up below the first floor on about the third terrace of the landscaping, halfway between the bottom floor of our building and the road below. This was good news. It could have landed on someone else's balcony, or gone through someone else's window.

In the afternoon, Larry reconnoitered the situation and determined the ground was entirely too wet, slippery and marshy to attempt a rescue. The next day we asked our relocation coordinator to phone the manager and tell her we would recover the wayward table on Saturday.

On Friday about 4:00 p.m., the skies opened up and the rain began. By the time we were ready to leave work, the downpour was in full swing. Looking up at the bridge heading toward downtown *Osaka*, we realized traffic was not moving. We made the decision to go home by way of *Kobe* and stop somewhere on the way for dinner. By the time we arrived in *Kobe*, we realized water was running from curb to curb and decided to forge on homeward without stopping.

Every street on the entire trek was awash. We had been told the open trench drains were preferred because they were better at moving large quantities of water. Not so. They had become so clogged with weeds and debris they were relatively useless in controlling the overflow situation, and we might as well have been trying to drive through the canals of Venice. Think Noah. Think ark. Think slow traffic. Think long, hard drive.

Three hours after leaving the site, we finally made our way into *Takarazuka*. Our only consolation was, had we taken our usual route through *Osaka* we would probably have arrived even later. As we ascended the final hill to our place, the rain eased up.

Saturday dawned—overcast, hot and steamy. Late in the afternoon, Larry checked the situation with the table. From our fifteenth-floor balcony, it seemed happily ensconced on its back, legs in the air in the same place it had originally fallen. He determined the ground was no longer a bog, so a rescue might be attempted.

Larry assembled his equipment: the rope he used to tie his surfboard to the top of the van and a mesh luggage strap in case he needed to remove the table legs and tie them together. Thus armed, we descended to the first floor to attempt recovery.

We walked around the building to get to a place directly above the location of the table. On the way, we passed three of the little boys who lived in our building (about eight years old) having a baseball game. We received their

47

usual exuberant greeting of, "Har-row!" We feared they might be the last friendly voices we would hear for a while.

Using his vast Boy Scout knot tying training, Larry firmly fastened the rope to the fence at the top. I was left with the coiled rope as lookout and backup in case emergency assistance might be required. Larry climbed over the locked gate and reached the stairs leading down to the second level terrace of the hill. After contemplating the potential hand and footholds on the second gate, he discovered it was, in fact, unlocked. He forged through the head-high undergrowth to a spot directly above the table. Fortunately the white color of the table contrasted enough with the green of the foliage to be able to be seen. Had it been a green table, the task might have been even more difficult.

For a few seconds Larry contemplated rappelling down to the table using the rope. However, since it was an old rope about the same thickness as a clothesline, and the path downward was not discernible from the top, he decided to try another tack.

He retraced his way up the steps and over the upper gate. Then he walked to the far end of the building where there were stairs leading to the street below. He descended until he was on the same level as the table. Then he climbed over the wall flanking the stairs and dropped into the brush below. His direction was clear—straight ahead.

A machete would have been handy as he fought his way through the jungle. The sounds of scurrying creatures could be heard around him. We had been told there were no snakes in the area. He hoped so.

He didn't encounter snakes, but there were bugs: gnats, flies, bees, beetles and mosquitoes. People might be small in Japan but the bugs were huge.

Pushing trees aside and avoiding drainage ditches along the way, he slowly made progress toward his goal. We had been watching "Ecochallenge" on the Discovery Channel, and the grueling conditions faced by those athletes encouraged him onward.

Thick plants of all kinds slowed his way. They also hid hazards. Like a foam beer cooler which he stepped directly into. It was filled with rainwater, so he extracted his foot with his pant leg soaked to the calf.

At last he reached the errant table. I coiled the rope and threw it down to his location. The table came along willingly. After a few days exposed to the weather, it was happy to return home. Larry was able to find a path to the upper level. So, with a firm grasp on the table, he ascended. He made his way back to the unlocked gate, climbed the stairs and lifted the table over the locked gate to my waiting arms. Then he made one last climb over the gate and was, once again, back safe on solid ground.

The table was returned to the atrium in the center of the apartment and reunited with the rest of the outdoor furniture. Another typhoon survived, and an exciting adventure had by all.

From Model to Scene...
And In Between

Rockwork
False rocks created from molded wire mesh, coated with Spraycrete (sprayed-on-concrete like the Gunnite used in swimming pools), sculpted into the desired shape and painted to resemble rock.

*   *   *   *   *

Larry

I always wanted to be a model maker. When I saw the film *20,000 Leagues Under the Sea* as a child, I hurried home and built the sets from scrap wood, old thread spools, cardboard and other junk I found around the house. My father only allowed me to use his coping saw, and I had to replace the ten blades I broke during construction. Some of those miniatures were stored in my bedroom; others made their way into the bathroom and became tub toys until they grew moldy and fell apart.

From set models, I graduated to the usual kits for cars, planes and boats. I refused to glue them together, however. It allowed me to change them from time to time. Unfortunately, when my mother tried to move them to dust, they tended to fall to pieces. She stopped dusting.

A few of my favorite car replicas survived into the first couple of years of our marriage. Lorna was a bit more inventive than my mother and purchased inexpensive display boxes for them. She could then dust the boxes without disturbing the fine works of art within.

Later, when I was working for an engineering firm in the petrochemical industry, 3/8" = 1'-0" scale models of refinery units were made to check the piping layout and find interferences or misfit equipment before the actual construction began. However, all I was allowed to do was attach pre-made green painted plastic cubes representing electrical equipment. No creativity was required.

In the 1970s, the increased use of CAD (Computer Aided Design) and the ability to do 3-D modeling within the computer made the need for actual physical models all but disappear. Very little three-dimensional miniature making remained, with the exception of one industry—Entertainment.

In this environment, both the almost forgotten arts of hand drafting and detailed model making were alive and thriving. While the architectural and engineering drawings for the USJ project were made in CAD, the art direction drawings were still made with pencil on vellum and many renderings and scale models were used for the attractions.

*   *   *   *   *

Creating the look, color and texture of scenes, sets and props (entertainment industry terms for buildings, walls, rocks, trees, and almost everything seen in the park) was not accidental. Each had been studied, discussed, often changed and finally approved by the art direction group.

It usually began with a rough concept sketch in pencil of an entire scene. After official acceptance, a color rendering was made of all or portions of the scene, and this was also approved. For complicated three-dimensional shapes like rockwork, a scale model was then carved out of Styrofoam blocks. The shape was "blessed," then painted and further detailed for final approval.

Models were made to serve several different purposes. The small-scale overall site model showing the entire park layout was created to be a sales tool and to encourage sponsorships. It was moved to the USJ Co. offices on the thirty-eighth floor of the *Osaka* World Trade Center and remained there. Others were used as construction aids to convey the desired look to the workers actually building or painting the scene.

The model for the *Jurassic Park* waterfall rockwork was extremely important since the GCs planned to laser scan it. The results of the scan were fed into a computer to create a 3-D image from which the full-size support steelwork and final construction shape was formed. The rockwork consultant spent months building the model of the main splashdown waterfall at *JP* to precise detail. Finally, not long after my arrival in Japan in the fall of 1998, it was ready to send.

The model was partially disassembled, crated and shipped to our offices on the twenty-eighth floor of the *Osaka* WTC. Upon arrival, the delivery company discovered the crates were too large for the building elevator. Even when uncrated, some sections would not fit. So, out came the Sawzall, and our beautiful miniature was "cut to fit."

51

I arrived at work the next morning to find pieces of waterfall and foam rocks piled haphazardly in the model room. Support legs had been sawn off the mounting tables, bracing was removed and parts were generally mixed up. We only had about a week before the GCs were to begin their laser scan. Stresh and I surveyed the mess and discussed the problem. There was no time to get model makers flown in from Hollywood to help, and since we were the only two relocated expats for the area, it fell to us. He had a Makita cordless driver. I had some metric wrenches and screwdrivers from the toolkit in the USJ rental car and my tools from home.

The first order of business was finding replacement legs, angle brackets, screws, etc. Being new to the neighborhood, we consulted the young relocation coordinator as to where we might find parts. She asked her father, who came up with two suggestions: *Tokyu Hands* (a do-it-yourself store) and the *Konan*.

So, armed with several maps borrowed from the relocation group, and an English translation of a Japanese father's detailed directions to each location, I began the mission.

First stop, the five story *Tokyu Hands* building in downtown *Osaka*. Just getting there was no small feat in cross-town traffic, remembering the correct side of the road and driving the relocation rental car. *Tokyu Hands* was disappointing. If we had needed camping gear, travel accessories, or anything for the hobbyist, this was definitely the place. I found no wood for table legs or usable hardware. There was, however, what appeared to be an entire floor devoted to *noren* (kitchen doorway curtains), but that would have to wait for another time. I left empty handed.

The trip to the *Konan* in *Amagasaki* was another hour's drive from downtown *Osaka* but proved to be much more productive. This store was not unlike a Home Depot, but not as well organized. It took several hours wandering around to finally locate all the needed parts.

Once back at the office, I enlisted Lorna to help organize the mess. While Stresh and I repaired table legs, Lorna unpacked and sorted the two-hundred or so bubble wrapped, carved foam pieces comprising the rockwork. Hollywood sent several pictures of the completed model, taken prior to shipment. With photos in hand, our job became very much like putting a 3-dimensional jigsaw puzzle together from the box top. Several foam parts were broken and some paint was missing. Our threesome completed the reassembly, applied touch-up paint and even added some plastic wrap to simulate a cascading waterfall, and still had a couple of days before GC scanning started.

Completed, the display was about twenty-two feet long by ten feet wide and five feet tall.

The GCs laser scanned the model the following week. Once in the computer, the shapes were used to make the full-size templates from which the rock forms of support rod and wire mesh were built.

Since our last-minute repairs were also included, this may have been the only instance where two facility people and a document controller actually influenced the look of anything at the park (a task jealously guarded by the art direction group). It's fun to speculate anyway.

*   *   *   *   *

About four months later, the same model was again moved, this time from the WTC to join the other attraction models sent directly to the on-site offices. However, unlike before, now there were plenty of hands to assist, and it went smoothly under proper art direction control.

Joining the *JP* model in the field office were ones of the *JAWS* piers, jetties, beach and hanging shark, the *E.T.* forest and home planet, the parks around the Main Lagoon, the sets for the *Animal Actors Stage* and the new *Peanuts* area.

Following these, another entire group of miniatures arrived. They were the training makettes, sized about twelve inches long by ten inches high and six deep. Each detailed a rock face, a block wall, a riverbank, a jetty, anything the GCs would be required to sculpt in concrete in the field. The resulting test piece, when scaled up to full size, would be twelve feet long by ten feet high by six deep. When it was announced the full size mockups would be fabricated in the dirt lot right behind our office, the staff was thrilled. Many, like Lorna, were office-bound and did not get on the construction site on a daily basis. The chance to see work in their backyard was a treat.

Steel base skids were brought in to make the completed mockups portable by forklift or crane. I-beam framework was covered with smaller bent rebar support and wire mesh to form the basic shapes. Finally, the Spraycrete was applied and the sculpting began, all under the close scrutiny of the rockwork consultant and his staff. The GCs got a chance to learn and practice their technique, and the consultant was able to give tips and suggest methods to improve the application. Finally when a mockup was completed to the art directors' satisfaction, it was moved to the site and placed adjacent to where the actual wall or rock face would be built as a sample for the final product.

I'm sure the high quality of the workmanship found in the park can be directly attributed to the practice the GC workers got carving these mockups to the high standards set by the rockwork consultant and art directors.

*   *   *   *   *

At the conclusion of the project, construction models are usually destroyed. Most have been pretty beat up anyway from all the moving around and rough treatment received during construction. However, in the final days, the rockwork consultant had the center section of the *JP* waterfall (the same one we had reassembled after the moving incident) crated and shipped back to his California office. He said, "I've never saved one of these before, but the job turned out so well I wanted to keep this as a souvenir. Besides, this one is really beautiful." I wonder if he ever looked closely to see all the little "fixes" Stresh, Lorna and I made.

Who knows, maybe I wasn't such a bad model maker after all.

On Being Foreign

Ohayo Gozaimasu (Oh-high-yō gō -zaye-mas)
Good morning (Literally, "It's early")
Konnichi wa (Koh-nee-chee wah)
Good day (Used from about 11:00 a.m. until evening)
Konban wa (Kohn-baan wah)
Good evening

*   *   *   *   *

Lorna

As I stepped out of the train into crowded *Umeda* station on my first solo trip, I was immediately enveloped in a dark ocean. Waves of blue-black hair, with occasional whitecaps, swirled and bobbed around me. Beneath this undulating sea, I could catch glimpses of equally dark clothing—black, navy and occasionally brown. With my reddish hair, Irish-pale skin, hazel-green eyes and wearing a bright blue jacket trimmed in hot pink, I felt like a resident of a multicolored Oz stepping out into Dorothy's black-and-white Kansas. My foreignness suddenly overwhelmed me.

When I talked to Larry about this experience, he said he had encountered it also, except he was tall enough not to feel as though he were drowning.

*   *   *   *   *

We grew up in Southern California, and ethnicity was a non-issue. I attended a college where around 30% of the student body was Latino, about 30% was African-American, another 30% was of European extraction and the rest were "Other" (Asian, Native American, etc.). That was our norm. I was accustomed to being around divergent people. The only constant was variety. Now we were thrust into a homogenous society. And we were "different."

Although it would have been considered terribly impolite for the Japanese to stare at each other, they seemed to have no reservations about doing so at *gaijin*. Quite the contrary. Before too long, we began to expect to see small children pointing at us wherever we went. And in public places, we became accustomed to being gawked at by kids and adults alike.

Since the *Hanshin Takarazuka* train station was at the end of the line, we were usually able to sit when traveling to downtown *Osaka*. However, we learned early to put Larry at the end of the seat rather than in the middle. Even if it were the last opening on the train, few Japanese were courageous enough to settle next to him. They would rather stand.

Because I was closer to their size, I guess I posed less of a threat. Usually someone would come along and take the spot next to me if it were available. However, it most often happened only when it was the last seat left in the car.

*   *   *   *   *

When we first looked at potential housing in Japan, we chose *Takarazuka* because it was not an expatriate environment. We wanted to live with the Japanese. Our apartment or *mansion* ("*mahn-shone*"—above average apartment) was located in a building of over three-hundred units. There were about seven or eight of these buildings climbing the hill above the city. Our *mansion* was perched at the very top. In all those buildings there were only four *gaijin*—and we were two of them.

On the floor below us was a director of the Ritz Carlton Hotel in *Osaka*. He was an American with a Japanese wife and two children.

The only other *gaijin* in our area was an Australian who lived in one of the buildings down the hill. He was also married to a Japanese woman and had a lovely little daughter. We met him at *Burger City* about a year after our arrival. (*Burger City* was the name of the hamburger shop owned by our friends the *Igos*.) The Aussie worked for a company which made beer equipment for restaurants. His product was much in demand in *Osaka*!

Other than those two men, there were no other *gaijin* on the mountain.

At first we were merely a curiosity. Then, apparently, word got around that we were working on the Universal theme park project because we became a bit like status symbols.

There were about five or six little boys in our building, around eight or nine years old. They were always playing ball in the large entrance area. After several months, when they learned we wouldn't bite, they would come rushing up to us whenever we came home, yelling, "HER-RO!" (Meaning: "Hello.") Then they would scamper off, laughing uproariously.

It appeared to us this activity served a couple of purposes. First, it informed anyone observing our encounter that they actually "knew" the resident *gaijin*.

Second, it also seemed to establish their knowing the proper word of greeting in English. We would respond to them as they ran off, "Hello." The entire time we lived there, we never carried on any more conversation with them than the same exchange of greetings.

*   *   *   *   *

There were also a couple of teenage girls living in our building. We'd occasionally see them on the elevator or in the parking structure. We would nod and greet them in Japanese in passing.

One of the young ladies worked at a restaurant we enjoyed in town. Whenever we would go there, even if we were not sitting at her station, she would make a point of stopping by our table and saying, "Hello." (Actually, she usually said "*Konban wa*," since this was the correct greeting for evening when we usually saw her.)

One night we had eaten dinner at the restaurant and were at the entrance counter paying for our meal. Apparently she spotted us from the back, because she raced between the tables to reach us before we left. Once she got to us, all she did was greet us in her normal manner. We later decided this ritual of hers was, in part, to show her friends and coworkers she was acquainted with the strange foreigners in town.

One day we decided to visit the Family Land amusement park and zoo near the train station in downtown *Takarazuka*. In order to ride on the rides or see the displays, it was necessary to purchase tickets. They came in groups of ten. We had a nice day, but in the end, we still had a few tickets left over. On the stairs as we exited the park, we encountered this same young woman and a friend entering. We said our usual, "*Konnichiwa*," and bowed. (It was daytime, for a change.) Then we offered her our unused tickets, since she was just arriving.

She first looked shocked, then bowed deeply several times and kept repeating, "*Arigato, arigato!*" ("Thank you, thank you.") You'd have thought we had given her a diamond ring, so profuse was her gratitude.

We kept repeating, "*Daijobu, do itashimashite*." ("It's okay, you're welcome.")

We weren't really sure whether she was trying to impress her friend with her "acquaintance" with the *gaijin* or with the generosity of the Americans who lived in her building. For whatever reason, she was happy, and so were we.

*   *   *   *   *

It was a very strange experience getting onto the elevator of our *mansion* with total strangers, and having them push the button for our floor. There were only two units on fifteen—ours and our next-door neighbors'. And we knew our neighbors. These people we had never met usually got off the elevator before we did, leaving us to ride the rest of the way to the 15th floor alone. It was quite obvious that everyone in the building knew where the Americans lived!

Not only did the people in our building know where we were, so, apparently, did the people in the building below us on the hill.

Our first Halloween in Japan, we hosted a party for the Universal team members who were in town. For some reason, there were quite a few people in *Osaka* that week. We sent out email invitations with complete and detailed directions on how to find our place.

Most everyone arrived, having easily located our building. However, a couple of people got off the bus one stop too soon. They ended up at the building directly down the hill from us.

We lived on the 15th floor, but this building had no 15th floor, so they knew they were in the wrong place. Fortunately they found someone and asked where the Collinses lived. "Oh, Corrin-san," the helpful resident of our neighbor building replied and pointed up the hill toward our place.

Of course, we didn't know anyone who lived in the building. And the little Japanese man, who spoke no English, didn't know us. But he recognized the name, and knew exactly where we could be found.

Apparently we were the subject of much local gossip.

✳ ✳ ✳ ✳ ✳

There were advantages to being foreign. We were not held to the same rigid standards of behavior to which the Japanese were expected to conform. It was assumed we didn't know any better. If we committed the unforgivable—like blowing our noses in public or failing to remove our shoes inside—we might be politely reminded. However, it wouldn't be held against us. After all, we were just dumb *gaijin*.

Another advantage was that English students often wanted to speak with us. Most Japanese English instructors had never lived in an English-speaking country and didn't really know what the language was supposed to sound like. They knew more grammar rules than I will ever learn in my lifetime, and could have passed written exams with ease. But if the language was spoken, they often failed to recognize the English words.

The main reason for this was the structure of the Japanese language. Each sound contains a consonant and vowel combination. A very few consonant sounds stand alone. In addition, there are consonants in English missing in Japanese—like "V" and "L" and "R." (There is a letter which could be either "L" or "R" but is actually pronounced somewhere between those two sounds and a soft "D.") One of the few stand-alone consonants is either "M" or "N."

There is also no emphasis in Japanese. Each syllable is pronounced with the same amount of stress.

So, students studying English liked hearing it spoken and were a little disappointed if foreigners attempted to talk with them in their own language.

When I was first learning to read Japanese, I began with restaurant menus. When I could figure out some of the names of the food, I decided to try to order a meal with my newly-acquired skill. (It was possible to place our orders in most restaurants without a smidgen of knowledge of the language, because there were photos of all the items printed on the menu. We could just point at what we wanted—and did for several months.)

I was ready. I had practiced for days. We entered the restaurant and were seated at our table. I opened the menu and found the items I knew there. I would impress our server by ordering in Japanese.

The waitress came to the table and I ordered my first item. "*Tamago*," I said confidently, knowing she would recognize it as "eggs."

"Eggs," she repeated as she wrote the order. This was perhaps the only server we ever encountered who understood and spoke perfect English. So much for my hard-won ability.

*   *   *   *   *

Looking different had advantages whenever I was lost—which was often. It seemed as though every time I found myself walking around confused, some charming Japanese person would approach me and offer (usually with gestures) to lend assistance.

The first time I attempted to locate a chiropractor recommended by friends, I took a map with me containing a diagram, the address and the phone number—in both English and Japanese. I followed the diagram to the building where his office was supposed to have been. However, when I arrived, I discovered he had moved. I found this out through the head shaking, bowing, pointing and gesturing of the two women who now occupied the space where the chiropractor had previously been. However, they offered to phone the number on my map and find out where he had moved.

After reaching the doctor, they marked my map to show his new office—up two more blocks and around the corner. With profuse thanks, I headed out on my quest again.

I walked the two blocks in the right direction and turned the corner. His office, according to the drawing and the numbers I had been given by the "office ladies," was on the fourth floor of building 7-18. Unfortunately the block I was on had three buildings of more than four floors, and none of the three had any numbers on them resembling "7-18."

I walked up and down the block several times trying to figure out which was the correct one. I studied my new map, retraced my route, and confirmed I had indeed found the right street. I checked the address again, and was as confused as ever. Finally, a little Japanese man came out of one of the buildings along the street and indicated he would like to help me. I showed him the marked-up map. I showed him the new address. He walked up and down the block a couple more times with me. He couldn't figure out which building it was either.

I had taken the cell phone with me on this trip in case there were any problems. My Japanese rescuer offered to call the office again and ask which building was theirs. (I was afraid to call myself because, although the chiropractor spoke perfect English, his staff did not.) I gave the man my phone and he called the number. There were several, "*Hai, hai*"s. ("Yes, yes."). Then he turned off the phone and pointed straight ahead. We had been standing in front of the correct building the whole time.

I was very grateful for his help, and was to discover it was not unusual for a stranger to give assistance—especially to a foreigner. I couldn't imagine an American being willing to take as much time to help to someone who looked as scary as we must have to the Japanese.

*　　*　　*　　*　　*

One memorable week, all the really tall guys on the project were in the office on business trips at the same time. We could never figure out how Universal was able to hire so many people over six-feet tall for one project. But they did.

At lunch one day, we all decided to go to the buffet restaurant on the 42nd floor to eat. The elevators in the *Osaka* World Trade Center were unusual for Japan in that they held about eight to ten people instead of the usual four to six.

The elevator stopped on the 28th floor. The doors opened to reveal two small Japanese businessmen, or "*salarymen*," in their dark suits, white shirts and ties. Their eyes bulged out, their mouths dropped open, and they cowered into the back of the elevator as the six VERY tall men and I entered. I may have been the only one in the group who wasn't intimidating. Had I been alone, I might have been too.

I'm not sure our Japanese co-riders breathed on the entire trip up to the 42nd floor. It was a good thing it was an express elevator!

Finding Beauty

Kyoto (kee-oh-toe)
The capital of Japan for about 400 years between 794 and 1185,
it is considered the cultural heart of the country.

*   *   *   *   *

Lorna
The Philosopher's Path

One Sunday in June of 1999, we boarded the train in *Takarazuka* for the one hour trip to *Kawaramachi*. We had been invited to join our former Japanese language instructor, *Maki*, to see her hometown, *Kyoto*.

She met us near the station. Because she had borrowed her father's car to drive us to the area where she lived, we first walked the few blocks to the garage where she had parked. "Garage" may be a misleading term. It was actually an opening in the side of a tall narrow building leading to two turntables, nearly filling the interior space. To the left as we entered were two cavities, each wide enough for one vehicle. A car was driven onto the turntable, rotated 90° to face the gap, then slowly accelerated onto a rack. The driver exited, and it was whisked out of sight. The mechanisms resembled large oval Ferris wheels or the kind of rotating hanging systems often seen at American drycleaners. The racks were about six feet above one another, so only short vehicles could be stored there.

"This is neat," I said. "Let's shoot a video."

So, as the racks started rotating, Larry began filming. When her car appeared in the opening, *Maki* entered and backed out onto the turntable. The attendant pushed a button, and the platform revolved until it was facing the street. *Maki* paid the attendant an exorbitant amount of money, and we departed for her home, already impressed with parking in *Kyoto*.

Maki lived with her parents at the northern end of the city near the beginning of the Philosopher's Path, a famous walk past temples and shrines along a river lined with beautiful trees. The atmosphere was of peacefulness and beauty.

Before walking the path, however, we visited her home. There were two structures on the property. The larger two-story one was her father's workshop. The smaller building contained his showroom on the first floor and their living quarters on the upper level.

Between the two buildings was a perfect little garden. It amazed me how so much charm could be packed into such small spaces to create peaceful, soothing oases amid the hectic pace of Japanese cities.

Maki's father had designed the second building with the eye of an artist. It combined modern materials with the very best of classic Japanese lines. When looking at one of these structures, it was hard to tell if it was really new, or if it had just been renovated. It sat in place as if it had always existed there and was a perfect setting to display his beautiful work.

As we entered, we noticed several unusual pieces of furniture. These were designed and built by *Maki's* brother who, like their father, was also an artist and craftsman. Then, we came to the showroom itself.

It was actually two rooms which could have doubled as formal tearooms. Around the outside, quite a few pieces of his remarkable lacquerware were displayed, featuring amazing shell and ivory inlay. The designs were based on traditional Japanese themes of nature: water, flowers, bamboo, birds and animals.

Mr. *Hattori's* work sold for between ¥400,000 and ¥8,500,000 (about $3800 to $80,000). *Maki* had given us a color catalogue from one of his shows with photos of his work. The pictures, though excellent photographs, didn't begin to capture the quality of the pieces. When I first saw the book, I had thought I might like to own a small box. In my usual way, however, I had managed to select one of the most valuable items. After I saw the prices, I decided I would need a car more when we returned to California. My favorite piece was 1.6 million yen (around $13,000). I didn't bring any back home with me, but that didn't diminish my appreciation for these extraordinary creations.

*   *   *   *   *

After visiting the showroom, we walked down to the stream, passing through *Cherry Blossom Lane*. This pathway along a canal only stretched for the equivalent of about three city blocks, but what a picture it was. The trees would only bloom for a couple of weeks in April. On this day, they were leafed out, lush and green. It was easy to imagine how impressive the walkway must be when overshadowed with lacy clouds of pale pink and white blossoms. What a glorious place it must have been to take one's daily constitutional.

The lane lead to the Silver Pavilion (*Ginkakuji*). Inside the temple grounds was a small volcano-like mound of perfect white sand set in a sea of the same material—equally white and artistically raked to resemble undulating waves. We were told that when the moon shone on this miniature mountain, it appeared to glow like silver.

The temple gardens were fabulous with numerous shaded paths and bridges, a waterfall and carefully planted and tended flower beds.

From the Silver Pavilion, we began walking toward the center of *Kyoto* on the official Philosophers' Path. This walkway followed a small stream and was lined with lawns and trees and benches. One could imagine meandering along, stopping from time to time to read or contemplate or simply to rest and enjoy the scenery. We took many photographs and most of them could have been framed.

Farther along the path were several more temples and shrines. One was a Buddhist temple with a pagoda rising high on the hill behind the main buildings. We climbed towards the pagoda, and then heard the rhythmic sound of a drum, followed by the low tone of the priests chanting. A service was in progress, and the deep timbre was soothing and restful, especially with the visual background of the gardens below. All the way up to the pagoda, we could hear the intonation of the chant. From the top, we looked out over *Kyoto*. The view, along with the sonorous cadence combined to create an unforgettable memory.

After visiting the temples, we went on to the *Gion* district at the southern end of the path. *Gion* was the foremost *geisha* area in *Kyoto*, and perhaps in all of Japan. Larry and I had read the book *Memoirs of a Geisha,* and had especially wanted to see the place. Images described in the book were preserved there. Wooden structures behind ancient gates were arranged in compounds, appearing as if they had existed there for hundreds of years. What had once been tearooms but were now restaurants still lined the small river.

In seeing this part of *Kyoto,* we were reminded of the beauty we had expected to find in Japan—and, at least on this day, did.

*   *   *   *   *

Hikone Castle

The following Saturday we took a guided tour of *Hikone* Castle. There were many feudal castles in Japan, but only three attained the status of historical treasures. Two of them were located in our area: *Himeji* and *Hikone*. The third, *Matsumoto* Castle, was near Tokyo. These three were special because each had its original *donjon* or main tower intact from the time it was built. Other castles in Japan (including *Osaka* Castle) had been destroyed and rebuilt.

Hikone Castle had just completed its second restoration in its 300-year history. Imagine, renovating only every 100 years.

Our entourage was made up of several members of the Universal team and friends from our church in *Kobe*. We took the train north beyond *Kyoto* to the *Hikone* station near Lake *Biwa*. There we were met by more tour guides—a total of four for our group of about thirty. We learned the history of the castle, and took a walk through town. Then we were allowed to go our own way for lunch, and told to meet for our tour of the castle afterward.

*   *   *   *   *

At lunch, Larry had an "only-in-Japan" experience. (We would have similar experiences again, but this was the first.) As Americans, we were accustomed to having food prepared to order. In Japan, food was served only the way the particular restaurant made it. There were no special orders, and getting it your way was never an option.

We each ordered the lunch plate. Following the meal, the children and ladies were presented a small scoop of green tea ice cream. Larry asked if he could purchase dessert as well. Our translator conveyed the request, so we were certain there was no misunderstanding due to language.

The restaurant owner was adamant. Ice cream was for children and ladies only. Even though they carried the ice cream, it was impossible to purchase it separately. That's the way it was served there. I gave him mine as did one of the other gals in our party who didn't care for it. But it was one of those instances that just wasn't logical to us.

*   *   *   *   *

The view from the summit of the hill where the castle stood looked out over the city of *Kyoto* and over Lake *Biwa*.

Hikone's architecture was very interesting. It was built in much the same style as *Osaka Castle*. The entrance, through a dry moat, had a collapsing bridge that could be dropped in the event an enemy had been able to get over the wet outer moat. The steps leading up to the castle were very steep and uneven, and were also designed to prevent easy access to the fortress.

Our tour guides were very knowledgeable, making the experience an interesting history lesson for the adults as well as the kids.

After exploring the castle, we strolled down to the formal gardens. These may well have been the most impressive ones we saw in Japan. Besides the trees, grasses, flowers, streams, small lakes and bridges, these also featured swans, cranes, egrets and herons in the trees, swimming in the lake and perched around the grounds.

In the center was a charming teahouse where we enjoyed a traditional tea ceremony. We were first served green tea *mochi*. *Mochi* is pounded rice used as the basis of many Japanese sweets. A small ball of warm *mochi*, with a bit of sweet red bean paste in the center, had been rolled in a coating of green tea powder and finely ground sugar. This morsel, about the size of a donut hole, was served wrapped in a delicate rice paper package. As with most everything in Japan, the appearance was as important, if not more important, than the taste. Many of the Americans in our group didn't like the texture of the sticky rice, but Larry loved it and I enjoyed it as well.

Our tour guides showed us the proper way to lift the teacup, turn it, drink from it, "slurp" at the end, admire the artistry, check for the artist's mark on the bottom, turn the cup again and replace it on the *tatami* mat. We were also shown the correct way to kneel, bow to the server, pass the sweets while bowing to each other, and acknowledge the server when the cups were collected at the end of the ceremony. Larry and I both enjoyed the special thick green tea reserved for the tea ceremony. But some in our group did not. We had experienced it before during the visits of the Japanese students in our home and knew what to expect.

During the ceremony, we also were able to appreciate the charm of the garden. The Japanese sense of the aesthetic in nature is nowhere more evident than in the arrangement of a perfect garden. And to top it off, as we were sitting and admiring the view, a blue heron took flight from the trees, circled across the lake several times, and finally came to rest on a post in the water where he seemed to pose so we could take his picture. I'm not sure how the folks who work there planned that one, but it was spectacular.

The day ended with the train ride back to *Kobe* recalling the experience with our friends and feeling very blessed to have gained an appreciation for the great beauty for which Japan is so justifiably famous.

Nihon Cowboy

Nihon (Nee-hohn)
Noun meaning "Japan" or adjective meaning "Japanese" (Old
version was "Nippon")

      *   *   *   *   *

Lorna

The "*Nihon* Cowboy" was arriving in *Osaka*! He was one of the Area 3 show producers, and one of the most fascinating people on the project.

He was born and raised in Japan. His family owned a hand-made brush company and as the oldest child, and only son, he was expected to inherit the family business. But, as he explained to me, "From the time I saw my first film when I was five years old, I told my family I was going to Hollywood to make movies." That desire never waned, and his family supported his dream. Even in post-war Japan, this encouragement was unusual.

He saved his money while attending high school in Japan and, following his graduation, purchased a one-way ticket to Los Angeles. "I didn't have enough money for a round trip. But it didn't matter. I wasn't going back anyway," he said. He arrived in California knowing no one and not speaking the language. But he had a dream.

He applied to UCLA, but lacking adequate English skill, was rejected. So he enrolled at a junior college, got a job and found a cheap room to share. "The next year I applied to UCLA, and was rejected again. But I still had my dream. I kept working on my English and going to junior college. The following year, after earning my AA degree, I was finally accepted at UCLA and could study film making for real."

He found what he really enjoyed was creating sets. (In fact, a short film on which he was the production designer won an Academy Award.) He got assignments on several projects. Then he was asked to do some larger jobs including staging shows for Japanese theater companies touring the US, where his Japanese language skills plus his artistic ability proved to be a valuable combination.

Once he arrived in the US, he never looked back. He fancied himself a cowboy—dressing all in black (a la Johnny Cash), always wearing cowboy boots and sometimes a black cowboy hat.

$*$ $*$ $*$ $*$ $*$

When the opportunity to work on a theme park in Japan came along, he was enthusiastic.

In every group there seems to be one person who is able to "procure" whatever is needed. The Cowboy was the person on the USJ team. When we had to test how various materials would react to being in water, he unearthed a huge aquarium on the backlot. When specialized props were required for our shows, they magically appeared in the office. We were trying to locate some old, beat-up boats for the *JAWS* lagoon, and the Cowboy came through there too. No one ever questioned precisely where these things came from. We were just grateful to know when we needed something, it showed up. And he was the source.

Because of his bilingual skill, he was a very popular figure among the general contractors (GCs). He facilitated many conversations between *Osaka* and Hollywood early in the project. And he was adept at explaining in ways both groups could comprehend.

$*$ $*$ $*$ $*$ $*$

He was most anxious to make a trip to Japan for the project, but time passed and he wasn't scheduled for a business trip. Finally, in October of 1998, he planned a vacation to visit his family. Once he knew he would be in Japan, we received a call.

"Hi, I'm coming to *Tokyo*. But I'll also go down to *Osaka* for a couple of extra days. I want to visit the office and meet everyone, and I'd really like to see the site." This referred to the place where the park would be built.

At this point, the USJ offices were all in the *Osaka* World Trade Center (WTC). From our 28th floor aerie, we could look out over *Osaka* Bay and see the jobsite, but none of the Hollywood team had yet been able to visit the actual location. The old metal plant which previously occupied the area had been dismantled and removed, but hazardous material (heavy metals and leftover WWII ordinance) was still being removed from one corner, and additional preparation was required before we would be able to move our offices there to begin construction.

"I'm sorry. They won't let anyone on the site yet, and we don't know when the clean-up will be completed," I replied. "But we'd love to see you and the GCs would too! Let us know the dates."

As soon as his trip was set, he called again. "I have my tickets, but the company won't cover my expenses. Do you know of anywhere I can stay?" (He would still technically be on vacation.)

"We have a guest room in our apartment. You're welcome to use that. And you can carpool to the office with us," I offered.

"Great!" he answered. "Do you think we could go to dinner with some of the people I've been talking to on the phone while I'm there?"

"Since we have the 'party house' we could plan a dinner party for your first night in town," I suggested.

"Are you sure?" he asked.

"We'd love it," I answered.

"That would be wonderful."

"I'll ask all of the Hollywood gang who are here and some of the Japanese team if you let me know who you'd like to have."

"Great, I'll email you a list."

Shortly thereafter, however, we started hearing he had talked to more of the *Takenaka* and USJ Co. people, and the size of the group grew.

"Hey, Cowboy," I said when I next talked to him, "we can host a big party since our place is large, but we live quite a distance from the WTC."

"Yes, some of the guys live in the opposite direction from you, and we've been talking about having dinner closer to the WTC so everyone can get together right after work."

"Sounds fine to us," I replied. "We want whatever works best for everybody."

As the time grew near, the number of people continued to increase. Soon all the GC and USJ Co. people were involved. Finding a restaurant large enough to hold that many was becoming a challenge.

Finally, the USJ Co. managers offered to arrange for one of the banquet rooms at the WTC and invited everyone in Area 3 who was in *Osaka*—the Universal Hollywood team, the GCs, and their own people. And they offered to pay for the whole party.

*　　　*　　　*　　　*　　　*

At last the Cowboy was on his way. He called from *Tokyo* to let us know when he would be arriving. And arrive he did.

69

On his first day in town, lots of meetings were scheduled so he could attend them. Unfortunately a couple became quite heated. This was early in the project when communication was still fraught with misunderstanding. And some of the American team hadn't yet adapted to the Japanese negotiation style.

By the end of the day, tempers were short and some were wondering if this party was a good idea.

Around 6:00 everyone began to arrive at the banquet room on the 42nd floor. It was arranged beautifully with the obligatory *sake* and beer as well as soft drinks for those who might be driving. There were several large tables covered in appetizer-style Japanese food. (*Yakitori, sushi, onigiri* and other delicacies.)

This was the first time we were able to meet with all the Area 3 design team members from Japan as well as some new faces from Hollywood. Within the first half hour or so, the same people who had been in heated discussions earlier were laughing together.

The party started in the usual Japanese manner. Speeches were given by all the managers—statements of confidence in the future of the project and the wonderful relationship we all expected to have. The certainty this park would be a boon to the city of *Osaka* and the people of Asia was expressed. And the competence and ability of all of the team members were extolled. After each toast, the crowd responded, "*Kampai!*" as they raised their glasses.

This was a critical moment as all of us were able to feel united in our common desire to produce the finest theme park in the world.

Seeing the camaraderie displayed in the room, I insisted a group photo be taken. There were a few grumbles, but eventually everyone agreed to pose. A waiter shot pictures with several of the cameras present.

The following morning, we went to the photo shop in the WTC to have our film processed. This particular store gave us a coupon for a free enlargement with each roll of film they processed. Since we had been taking lots of photos to send back to California, we had accumulated quite a few of these coupons.

Later in the morning when we picked up our prints, we discovered the group photo had turned out exceptionally well. Everyone was grinning and obviously having a good time. The teams were mixed, Japanese with Americans, arms around each other.

We used our coupons to have four enlargements made. These were ready later the same day, and we put them in inexpensive frames.

We presented one copy to USJ Co. in thanks for their sponsoring a wonderful party. We gave the second copy to the GC. The third was posted in the Area

3 offices in *Osaka*, and the Cowboy took the fourth back for the Area 3 offices in Hollywood.

All those photos remained prominently displayed during the remainder of the project. They were a tangible reminder of the optimism and enthusiasm we shared in the beginning. Many people in the photo became dear friends during the course of the job. Some of those friendships remain to this day.

At the end of the project, we brought the *Osaka* copy home with us. Whenever we look at it, we are reminded of a special evening and wonderful people.

*   *   *   *   *   *   *   *   *

Many of the team members had wanted to visit the jobsite, but had been told it wasn't safe enough yet. Nevertheless, the morning after the party, we were informed a bus would arrive at 9:00 to take whoever wanted to go to the site for a visit. The Cowboy's persuasion worked again! And once again, USJ Co. came through.

I stayed at the office because I hadn't been issued my steel-toed shoes yet, but Larry had his boots and went with the group. (All the big-footed Americans had purchased steel-toed boots in the US and taken them to Japan since they would have been unable to locate their sizes there.) Foot protection was definitely required on this visit.

Larry took his camera with him and shot the first of many photos of the jobsite. (All the site photos were sent to the project files when we left Japan because of the proprietary nature of some of the subject matter. Since the park was not yet opened at that time, the company did not want any information to get into competitive hands. It would be interesting to see them again now, but we assume they have been permanently archived.)

While wandering about, the Cowboy displayed his usual ability to find just the thing we needed. As he walked around through the dirt, he stumbled upon some old rusty pieces of metal including an old anchor. These were set aside to be used as props for the *JAWS* ride and the *WaterWorld* show.

After the trip to the site, the park began to seem real. Now there was an actual location where it would be, and some of the team members had been there. They found it easier to visualize their design ideas in a particular place.

We enjoyed having the Cowboy with us for the few days he was able to stay. He was the first, but not the last, member of the Hollywood team to stay in our guest room. But all too soon, it was time for him to return to Hollywood.

As it turned out, he was never able to relocate to *Osaka* and left the project before it was completed. But his contributions were legendary—and we have the photo to prove it!

Driving in Japan

Gombatte kudasai (Gum-bah-tay koo-da-sigh)
Good luck—please do your best.

✳   ✳   ✳   ✳   ✳

Lorna

We had thought driving in Scotland on vacation was a challenge. In Japan, Larry was not only driving on the left-hand side of the road in a car with right-hand drive, but there were lots of additional complications to deal with.

Since I refused to drive there, my wish for him was always, *"Gombatte kuda-sai!"* (Good luck!)

Maps

We must have had a dozen maps of the *Osaka* area. Most were in English. Every one was different. Streets were shown in the wrong places or missing altogether. One had route numbers but no names. Another had names but no route numbers. A third showed connections between expressways which, in fact, didn't connect. Some showed city names. Some didn't. Or they might have shown selected cities but not others—including fairly major ones.

We ended up using a combination of two or three maps when going anywhere. We had to wander around and locate a place once to be able to identify landmarks so we could get there again. Attempting to drive to places for the first time was a real headache.

One Sunday shortly after we arrived, we decided to attend services at the *Kobe Union Church,* recommended by our friend Kay. We allowed an hour and a half to get there. We had calculated the trip from our home in *Takarazuka* to the church to be about forty to fifty minutes. Four hours later, we gave up.

Both our city maps showed the church in the same place in downtown *Kobe.* Unfortunately, this was the location of the original building which had been sold years before. Had it been the correct spot, we'd have arrived in time for services. But, although we had just bought the maps, we discovered they were about nine years or more out of date.

The following week, we found a small detail map to the church in a book on living in *Kobe*. So we decided to give it another try. However, this map was intended for people arriving by train or bus and was missing a very key turn we should have made when driving. We finally found the church over an hour after services concluded, but we still weren't exactly sure how we got there.

The third week, we emailed the church, received turn-by-turn directions, and finally made it on time.

Street Names (or lack of same)

Few streets, except in *Kyoto*, actually had names. Most didn't. The intersections had names, but not the streets. There were also no house numbers as such. Buildings had numbers, but those were based on the order in which they were built and not their position on the block. Even main roads were sometimes named only for short distances. Then they sort of dribbled out.

Streets (or lack of same)

Few of the streets would have qualified as such in the US. Not many would have been considered respectable alleys. Most would be looked upon as cramped driveways. The lanes were narrower than a full-size American car. Few Japanese drivers paid attention to them anyway. We learned to identify a major thoroughfare, not because it was wider, but because it had an orange stripe down the center.

Also, few would have been considered safe by American standards. Along the sides there were most often uncovered trench drains, about six to ten inches wide and about three to four feet deep. They were usually filled with grasses and reeds and were not readily visible. Since the roadways were so narrow, it would have been very easy to drop a tire into one. In addition, when getting in or out of the car, it was necessary to step over them. Our fellow expats called them "*gaijin* traps." (*Gaijin* means "foreigner.")

In many places, trees or poles along the streets were actually in the streets, making them even narrower. On our route to *Kobe*, there was a huge boulder, as large as a Volkswagen, in the center of the road. The pavement split around it. Larry was told the original plan was to move the boulder, but the people who attempted it died. It was nicknamed the "Rock of Death."

On the same road was a tight spot with parking on both sides. Larry was sure the vehicle he was riding in wouldn't get through. But our American neighbor, who was driving at the time, told Larry to reach out and fold the side mirrors in. Then they crept, inch by slow inch, between the parked vehicles. After they had cleared them, they reached out, pushed the mirrors back into place, and continued on their way. When Larry asked if this was unusual, he was told it was quite common. In fact, newer model Japanese sedans had automatically retracting mirrors, activated by a button inside.

Parking (or lack of same)

Parking was hard to find in many areas, but was usually available in the centers of larger cities. Lots could be identified by large signs featuring either a green or blue "P" located near the entrance. They were most often multilevel parking structures. And they were expensive. We went to *Kobe* for dinner and shopping one evening, and the parking cost ¥1000 (about $9.00). We parked the car on another day for less than an hour. The fee: ¥600 (about $5.50).

However, many people simply made their own parking places—in the streets, on the sidewalks, or wherever they saw an opening. The scene was reminiscent of San Francisco. Drivers sometimes double or triple parked. They just turned on their emergency flashers while still in the lane, left their engines running, got out and zipped into the nearest convenience store, or to buy a beer or cigarettes from one of the street vending machines, or to make a delivery. We were told this was perfectly legal, and we never saw the police cite anyone for doing it.

Signage (or lack of same)

We were extremely fortunate the Japanese had added English words to the traditional *kanji* characters and adopted Arabic numerals for their road signs. International symbols were used far more often than we were accustomed to in the US. This meant identification for major roadways could sometimes be found.

However, a sign might show an upcoming turn. Then, after we'd made the turn, all references to the route disappeared. Or a major highway might only be identified by signs visible when looking down the road—after passing it. Signposts were often placed at the point of the turn, so there was no warning; and there was no "going around the block" to get back to where we had been.

Occasionally there was a dedicated left or right turn only lane. Actually, there wasn't an additional lane added. The lane we were driving straight in became the dedicated turn lane. Unfortunately, these were usually marked only on the street as we got to them, so there was no time to change lanes and avoid making the turn. However, everyone just changed lanes anyway or went straight.

Most directional signs were not lighted at night. There were bright lights and flashing letters on every business establishment, including rotating emergency beacons. This made reading the unlighted directions after dusk nearly impossible. And they were frequently hidden behind signals and trees.

Duplicated Numbers and Names

One of our great frustrations in following directions was that route numbers and route names were duplicated—often within the same city and within a kilometer or so of each other. One night we were looking for Route 176 and followed the signs, but ended up in an entirely different location than "our" Route 176 would have taken us. We also found at least three Route 2s and several Route 171s. Since these were all highways we depended on, it became quite confusing.

Not Reading the Language (our problem)

It is hard enough to try to navigate in a strange American city with a fairly up-to-date AAA map, but not understanding the words on many of the signs made the task monumental. Thank goodness accommodation had been made for foreigners in the tourist areas by adding some English to the signs and by using international symbols. However, there were often times when just being able to read the Japanese might have been a great help. Our own lack of fluency in this area further complicated an already difficult process.

Locating Specific "Addresses" (or not)

Addresses in Japan were difficult—even for the Japanese. They started out with the prefecture (like the county or state). In our case: *Hyogo-ken.* Those areas were further divided into cities. Ours was *Takarazuka-shi.* ("*Shi*" meant "city.") Then the cities were divided into administrative districts called "*chome*" (chō-māy). We were in *3-chome* (*san-chome*)—the 3rd district. At a lower level, there were neighborhoods within the *chome* with their own designations. Ours was "*Sumiregaoka.*" Next came the specific building number and apartment number. Our building was 2-1 and our apartment number was

#1515. Postal codes were also used, which must have been of some use to the post office. But they didn't appear to have any logical order either. Ours was 665-0847.

So our address was:

Hyogo-ken, Takarazuka-shi
3-chome, Sumiregaoka, 2-1 #1515
665-0847

Now the challenge became how to find one of these addresses in a strange city for the first time on our own.

One Saturday evening we were invited for a pizza party at the home of one of the Universal people. We had been there once before, and Larry felt certain he could locate the place again. We made our way to *Suida* (the city) just fine and recognized several of the local landmarks. Then we spent an hour and a half driving around trying to spot the building. We finally had to phone and have someone come down to one of the landmarks to direct us. Even a gal who had lived in Japan for five years, read and spoke perfect Japanese and had a map, got lost!

Direction? What Direction?

Since most of Japan was covered with mountains, many of the streets and roads followed what must have been animal trails conforming to the contour of the land. They changed direction. Often.

Coming home one night we missed a turn. We realized our mistake and tried to "go around the block" to face the correct direction. An hour and a half later, we were back at the same place from which we had started.

The reason we got lost so easily was because all the roads we took changed direction so many times we were both completely turned around.

We subsequently bought three small compasses. Larry attached one to his watchband and I clipped another to the strap on my bag. We put the last one in the car. They helped.

The Adventure Continued

Fortunately, Larry enjoyed driving and saw this as another exotic adventure. I, on the other hand, found it far too intimidating. Being the passenger and navigator was challenge enough for me. Somehow we usually managed to get where we wanted to go and were able to laugh about it when we didn't.

Groundbreaking

Groundbreaking
The act or ceremony of breaking ground to begin a construction project

✳   ✳   ✳   ✳   ✳

Lorna

One of the first milestones of every construction project is the ground-breaking ceremony. This is when the first shovelful of dirt is turned on the site where construction will begin. For Universal Studios Japan (USJ), the occasion was October 28, 1998.

The big party for the Groundbreaking Celebration for USJ wasn't held at the real location because there was too much mud to accommodate a large crowd. All the local VIPs and media had been invited, so it was important to keep them clean and dry.

Instead, a small tent was erected in a cleared area on the actual site, and a Shinto ceremony was held there earlier in the afternoon featuring a traditional blessing by the local priests. Only a few of the highest ranking people from USJ Co., USI and the general contractors (GCs) plus a select number of press and officials from the city of *Osaka* were invited to the religious observation. The first shovelful of dirt was turned with great pomp and a sense of triumph. We later watched news clips of the ceremony on TV.

Until the day before, we weren't certain we'd be allowed to attend the large celebration. It seemed there were too many people and too few tickets.

Late the afternoon of the event, we were told there were tickets for the expats and their spouses. But when we left the office to catch the subway, the office manager and relocation team still remained, unable to go with us. Fortunately, one of the Hollywood gals, in town to help with this production, got them in by letting them use tickets for people who didn't show up. She said some names were very strange if matched with the individuals present. The highlight of my evening was seeing the group arrive. I had been feeling guilty and sad leaving them behind.

The party began at 5:30 p.m. across the bay from the jobsite on the grounds of the *Suntory* Museum. We arrived and were given our identification. Well, Larry was issued an ID card. I was handed a blue ribbon. I asked someone what the significance of the blue ribbon was. She said, "Wife." It was strange, however, as some of the other wives received the same ID cards as the guys. It was especially irritating to me since I was working on the project. I think the Japanese folks doing the check-in were confused by all the *gaijin*. They were also distributing receivers for the translation of the ceremonies into English. Neither of us was given one of those. Fortunately, Stresh and his wife received two and said they would share.

Champagne was being served as we arrived. There were also waiters circulating with Japanese-style canapés. There was excited conversation and meeting and greeting of friends and coworkers. Three enormous screens showed scenes from the various Universal pictures featured in the park.

This was an occasion when the Japanese and American teams could socialize away from the work environment. Since it was a festive event, everyone was relaxed and happy. A feeling of good will and camaraderie was very much in the air.

The formalities began with traditional speeches given by various Japanese officials, followed by welcoming addresses from members of Universal Studios management. Each speech was translated for the segment of the crowd who didn't comprehend the language of the speaker. All were acclaimed by cheers. Fortunately the orations were short. Then the entertainment began.

First a video from Steven Spielberg was shown. He told the history of the Universal theme parks and sent congratulations on the beginning of this one. At the end of the film, a cloud of smoke billowed up, and the robot from *Terminator 2* was raised from below the stage and began shooting over the audience. The figure was about fifteen feet tall, and the sound and laser effects were very impressive. Then, out of the smoke, stepped Arnold.

He almost didn't make it, however. Until a few days before, Spielberg himself had been scheduled to attend. At the last moment, he bowed out. Schwarzenegger and his family were vacationing in Hawaii when the Universal Marketing team located him. He agreed to hop on a plane to *Osaka*. However, it wasn't until he reached *Kansai* Airport that anyone realized he was missing his passport. It was at home in California.

There was much bureaucratic scrambling to get him into the country. The proper permissions were granted, the necessary stamps obtained, and he was finally allowed to leave the airport.[7]

---

[7] A year or so later, a Japanese official was forced to resign when it was discovered he had kept the original paperwork with Arnold's signature as a souvenir.

He was taken to the hotel with very little time before the ceremonies began. Fortunately he had a leather jacket from the film with him. But he was missing his trademark sunglasses. One of our lighting guys had a pair that would do, and he lent them to the Terminator for the show. They were never returned, and the now glasses-less victim spent days retelling and embellishing the story for all who would listen.

Once on stage, Arnold made a speech which drove the interpreter crazy. Everyone was supposed to be speaking from a script, but he began to adlib, and the translator started giggling. The audience joined her amusement, and the whole thing was well received.

When he finished, the lights went out, and two helicopters flew in with their searchlights panning the area. At the same time, the soundtrack from the movie E.T. was heard over the loudspeakers. As the volume increased, it became clear the choppers were searching for the alien. There was suddenly a loud whirring noise and a space ship began to rise from one end of the guest area. Then, through a cloud of smoke, E.T. himself appeared, waving to the crowd.

The wife of the Area 2 project engineer was a great fan. We had been told ahead of time where and when E.T. would appear. So we sent her to a spot where she could see him up close. After the show was over, she was allowed backstage to meet E.T., shake his hand and have her picture taken hugging him. It was a highlight of her stay in Osaka.

After E.T.'s appearance, fireworks began. The pyrotechnics team used a low-level kind to be featured in the nighttime lagoon show in the park. The colors varied from any I had ever seen before: pinks, blues, light green and yellow as well as silver and gold. The explosions were close to the audience, quite different than watching from a distance. They were spectacular.

Then the VP/CEO gave a delightful toast to the success of the park. Glasses were raised, and, "Cheers!" and, "Kampai!" echoed through the crowd.

The toast was followed by the dinner service. The Hyatt catered the event, and the fare was delicious. There were about seven food stations serving both Japanese and American cuisine including a spectacular array of desserts. Larry, following his motto of, "Life is short, so eat dessert first," started there. Then he moved on to main dishes, salads, etc. He finished up with his "real" dessert. Larry was content.

A couple of bars were in operation. [Universal was owned by Seagrams at the time.] Fortunately, there was also juice, ice tea and coffee for the non-drinkers.

As we exited, we were each given a commemorative gift. I knew what was in the packages because I had spent an afternoon the week before helping to wrap them.

Japanese wrapping is an art unto itself. The paper is positioned diagonally and must be lined up and creased just so, a bit like *origami*. The people in charge decided my job would be limited to attaching red ribbons and Universal stickers to the presents—after they were swathed in paper by those who were skilled at doing so. It was a wise decision on their part.

The press received *Hoya* crystal paperweights of the Universal globe, engraved with the date. The rest of us were given pocket watches, also engraved, including fobs and wooden stands for display—nice mementos of the evening.

We had experienced frustration with relocation issues and the resignations of several key project people. This event provided a much-needed change of pace. The spirit of hopefulness and excitement was re-generated for all of us, particularly the expatriates.

This celebration made us feel as though the project had finally started. It had become real. There seemed a greater sense of camaraderie among the team—American and Japanese—than before. Now, at last, we were ready to build USJ.

Dote-san

Hashi-oke (ha-shee-ō-kay)
Chopstick rest. They may be made of many materials: porcelain,
wood, plastic, ivory, etc. The designs are usually from nature:
leaves, animals, fish or branches.

*　　*　　*　　*　　*

Lorna

Since we had been warned not to expect to visit a Japanese home, the invitation for dinner at *Hidetoshi Dote's* (pronounced "dō-tā y") house early in our stay came as a surprise.

Dote-san was the head of Information Technology (IT) for *Takenaka* and was one of the small group of general contractor (GC) people with office space in the *Osaka* World Trade Center (WTC) when we first arrived. Although each group had separate suites, *Dote-san* spent most of his time loitering in the USI office space. Noting he had a sense of humor, I began teasing him about this habit.

"*Dote-san*, I know this will come as a shock to you, but you're NOT a member of the USI team. You really work for *Takenaka*. It isn't like a sports club you can join, and hanging around here all day won't make it happen."

He feigned surprised. "Really? I thought maybe no one would notice."

"I'm afraid it doesn't work that way."

Then he would laugh and wander off, only to reappear again shortly with a new matter of "business."

Dote-san was among the people invited to our first party on *Respect for the Aged Day* on September 15, 1998. He came and had a good time.

When we held our Halloween party in October, he was one of the first to accept. Once again, he had fun.

Then we planned our Christmas party for early December, and more of the *Takenaka* people attended, including the people who had visited California during Larry's early days with Universal.

We asked everyone to bring a "white elephant" gift worth no more than ¥1000 (or $10). The gifts were used for a "pirate" gift exchange where they were chosen, unwrapped and "stolen" up to three times until the final owner was determined. Our Japanese guests were a little confused at this odd way of giving presents, but soon got into the spirit of the game.

After having several other desirable gifts snatched away from him, *Dote-san* opened a Tee-shirt he particularly liked. He immediately donned it over his own shirt. Since he seemed so attached to it, no one had the heart not to let him to keep it.

Hatenaka-san allowed one of his sons to select the package to open when it was his turn. The little guy very deliberately made his choice, carefully removed the wrapping and revealed a clock. I have no recollection of whether it was a wall clock or table clock or if it were decorative or plain because he clutched it to his chest as if it were a great treasure. During the ensuing exchanges, several folks threatened to steal the clock from the child, but no one actually did. It went home with him, and the party was a complete success for the whole family.

*   *   *   *   *

After he had visited our place several times, the invitation for a meal in *Dote-san's* home arrived. Of course, we were delighted and accepted immediately.

We were a little concerned about finding the house since we would be driving. A few days before the scheduled date of our visit, *Dote-san* appeared at my desk with a large sheaf of papers. He had copied pages from a current Japanese street map book (much like our *Thomas Guide* in California), taped them together, highlighted the route, and added copious notes and sketches of landmarks along the way. He lived in *Kawanishi,* the next town to the north of us. But there were about seven pages of detailed directions, each about twenty inches long. These were the best instructions we had seen so far, and we were grateful for the effort he had made on our behalf.

Prior to our scheduled visit, the USI supervision hard hats arrived in the office. Ours were metallic gold with the USJ logo on the front—the only ones on the site that color. They had been labeled with our individual names. Each craft group on site had different colored helmets: electricians, plumbers, steelworkers, etc. could be easily identified at a distance by their blue or white or yellow hats. *Takenaka, Kajima* and *Obayashi* supervisors also had helmets in distinctive shades.

When *Dote-san* spotted the opened box on the office manager's desk, he asked, "Well, where's mine?"

83

"*Dote-san*, remember, you belong to *Takenaka*," I reminded him. "These are for the USI team."

He pouted, then brightened and said, "I'll just talk to the construction manager."

"You do that," I replied.

The day of our anticipated visit finally arrived, and the maps and directions proved to be as accurate as we had hoped. Following the highlighted yellow path, we discovered notes such as, "*Daiei* sign right side." And, sure enough, there was the by-now-familiar bright orange circle with the white lettering. In another place was a notation, "seven story pink apartments straight in front" with a sketch next to it. Just as described, we looked ahead, and there was the structure appearing much like the sketch. So it went through every twist and turn in the typical Japanese city.

Our only concern was locating his house when we turned onto his street. He had said it was the fifth one from the far corner, but we weren't completely certain we'd be able to identify it. We needn't have worried. When we turned on to his block, we noticed something sticking up above the level wall separating the houses from the road. As we got closer, we began to laugh. Displayed proudly atop the bricks next to the entrance gate was a shiny new USI helmet—complete with "*Dote*" on the back.

He stepped through the doorway beaming in triumph. He was finally—if unofficially—a member of the USI team. Then he grinned conspiratorially. "It's a secret," he whispered as he burst into chuckles of glee.

Once inside his modern home, we were greeted by his wife, *Michiko*. (She would also have been called "*Dote-san*" in Japanese since the honorific "san" has no gender.) She was a gourmet cook and had prepared an elegant dinner, obviously intended to appeal to our western palates. We enjoyed the food and the company.

We discovered they had previously lived in the US. Their oldest daughter, *Yoko*, had been a little girl there and spoke some English. At the time of our visit, she was a drummer in a rock band.

Their second daughter, *Yuko*, was a baby when they returned to Japan, so she had less conversational ability. She was quite shy and self-conscious about the quality of her English compared to her sister. *Yuko* and her brother would attend our *Hanabi Taikai* (Fireworks Festival) party the following August. With all the other young Japanese people in attendance, she seemed much more at home there.

The son, *Shunsuke*, was considerably younger than the girls and seemed a bit confused at all the foreign sounds he was hearing.

I made the mistake of admiring *Michiko's hashi-oke* (chopstick rest). I mentioned I was collecting them during our expatriate period. At the end of the meal, she presented me with the one I had been using. When I tried to refuse her offer, she insisted. It is now part of my collection, and I remember her fondly whenever I use it.

We enjoyed our evening with the *Dotes*, and *Dote-san* became a regular guest in our home for the rest of our stay.

*   *   *   *   *

One day *Dote-san* (he was always called that for business) dropped by my office at the jobsite.

"My colleague, *Okada-san*, is studying English with *Maki* (our lead translator). Besides learning to speak the language, he would like to meet some Americans. May I introduce him to you and Larry?"

"Of course, we'd love to meet him."

A little while later *Dote-san* returned with his friend and introduced us. We had recently seen the charming Japanese movie *Shall We Dance* and had loved it. The film, about a Japanese businessman who secretly defies the cultural norm to learn ballroom dancing, remains one of my favorites.

After the formal Japanese bow and introductions, *Okada-san* raised his left hand and placed his right at waist height a few inches in front of his body, then began moving gracefully across the floor. "Shall We Dance?" he said.

It was fortunate I knew the reference to the film and told him how much I had enjoyed it. After seeing the movie, he and his wife had begun ballroom dancing. It had become quite a passion for him.

We exchanged a few sentences, then the two men left the office.

A few days later *Dote-san* phoned me.

"*Okada-san* would like to take you and Larry to dinner," he announced. "And he would like you to choose an American restaurant."

"That would be lovely," I replied, trying to think of a restaurant he might like. "When would he like to do it?"

"Next Friday night," was the answer.

"Oh, dear, I'm afraid we have another engagement that evening," I replied.

"That is too bad. We have many meetings and *Okada-san* will be going on a long trip soon," *Dote-san* responded with disappointment. "That was his one free evening."

I sensed that *Okada-san* was pretty important, and *Dote-san* didn't want to disappoint him.

Our previously scheduled engagement was an open house at the Foreign Buyers' Club (FBC) on *Rokko* Island near *Kobe*. We were invited, along with the rest of their customers, for dinner on the large patio behind the store. They were importing steaks from a different Australian supplier, and wanted all of us to try the new products. In addition, they would be barbequing chicken and sausages. And there would be side dishes and desserts, all prepared with ingredients sold in the store. The cost was minimal by Japanese standards. The chief appeal for us was that most of our friends would be attending.

Wait a minute.

"*Dote*-san," I began, "if *Okada-san* really wants to meet some Americans, the place we are going on Friday would be perfect." I went on to describe the event, and to emphasize the large number of Americans likely to be in attendance. I was also certain that the food would be pretty standard American fare, giving *Okada-san* a chance to sample our cuisine.

"I'll check with *Okada-san*," he said, "and I'll let you know. But this sounds like the perfect solution." He called back a short time later with the word that *Okada-san* would be delighted to join us.

On Friday evening after work, we met the two men at the *Rokko* Island train station and showed them the way to FBC. As we neared the building, the tantalizing scent of barbeque smoke assailed us. When we arrived, the place was packed with people, mostly Americans, but some Japanese as well. Many of those in attendance were bilingual.

We introduced our guests to a number of our friends, and *Okada-san* had the chance to practice some of his newly-acquired English.

The steaks were wonderful, and the rest of the food equally tasty. *Okada-san* appeared to be having a great time. He spent part of the evening speaking with a Japanese employee of FBC. He had a lot of questions for her about working with and for the Americans. I guess he liked the answers.

From then on, whenever *Okada-san* had a meeting at the jobsite, he made a point of stopping by my office before he left. *Dote-san* had adapted to my American style of greeting everyone with a hug and bidding them farewell in the same manner.

Okada-san followed suit. On one occasion, he arrived and we spoke for a few minutes. When it was time for him to depart, he walked around to my side of the desk to collect his by now customary good-bye hug.

After he left, *Chie*, the other gal in Document Control, remarked, "You know, I'll bet the only time he's hugged is when he comes here. Japanese don't do that. And I think he really likes it." He certainly seemed to since he always went out of his way to make sure he didn't leave without one.

Okada-san was present at the next party we gave, along with several other *Takenaka* folks. At various times, their wives and other family members accompanied them. Everyone felt comfortable, and our home in Japan became the gathering place we had envisioned.

*   *   *   *   *

After returning to California, we remained in contact with many of the *Takenaka* group.

The fall after our return, we received a surprise phone call.

"Hello, this is *Hide* (Pronounced *Hee-dāy*)." Since we were no longer in a formal business relationship, he was letting me know first names were now acceptable on both sides.

"Hi, *Dote-san*, where are you?"

"I am in Tokyo, but I will arrive in Los Angeles on Friday."

"Wonderful! How long will you be here? Will we be able to see you?" There were too many questions for a long distance call.

"I have meetings in Los Angeles on Monday. I will fly to San Francisco on Tuesday for a conference. Then I will go to Las Vegas for a convention."

"Would you be able to come to our house?" I offered.

"I would love to come see you," he answered. "Is it okay?"

"It would be great!" I responded. "Can you stay the whole weekend?"

"I could if it is all right with you."

"I'll email you a map and directions," I replied.

He arrived Friday evening, and we had a wonderful two days catching up on all the news and showing him our area of the country. All too soon, it was time for him to depart.

"I hope you'll come back again," I said.

"I hope so too," he answered.

*   *   *   *   *

Dote-san comes to the US often. And when he does, he always gets in touch and visits when he can. It's as though he has finally become part of the USI team, if only as a member of our extended family.

87

Raouf

Haori (How-ree)
The jacket worn over a kimono. These are frequently painted or embroidered, and their long sleeves are used as pockets.

*　　　　*　　　　*　　　　*　　　　*

Lorna

Raouf Iskander was the project architect for Area 2. He and his partner *Antoine[8] and their dog *Kobe* landed in *Osaka* on August 10, just over a week after our arrival. Like survivors cast adrift on a desert island (or in a strange culture), we immediately bonded.

Raouf and I were both huggers. Japan was an extremely undemonstrative country. It was socially unacceptable to display affection in public. For both of us, this meant a challenge to our habits. However, we found one another.

Upon arriving in the office, we often shared friendly hugs in greeting, and did the same when leaving. Since we were in the American area, the Japanese seemed to accept our behavior.

Raouf was a real "people person." He wallpapered his cubicle at the WTC with photos and notes from friends, team members and family. Larry and I enjoyed checking to see what was new.

Antoine also became a good friend. In the early days, there were many unresolved issues, and he was as involved as the rest of us in trying to get them sorted out. He spent a lot of time in the office on his way to or from one appointment or another.

In the first few months, we were together often since we didn't know many other people in Japan yet. And when problems seemed all but insurmountable, we counted on Raouf to be able to laugh at them—and convince us to follow suit.

*　　　　*　　　　*　　　　*　　　　*

---

[8] Names with an asterisk are pseudonyms, used because we were unable to locate the actual people

Shortly after Raouf's arrival, our relocation coordinator modeled in a *kimono* show and invited the Americans to attend. Antoine, Raouf, Larry and I plus another team member in town on a business trip managed to find our way together to the large department store in downtown *Osaka* and locate the correct floor. (Since none of us had much experience with written Japanese early in our stay, it was definitely a challenge.)

Before the show, we had a chance to visit displays of the vendors to admire their goods. There were fabulous *kimono*[9] in various weights of silk, many with embroidery and painted scenes. They were in every shade and color—from dark black, brown and navy through the earth tones of beige, ecru and shades of green, to soft pastels and vivid red, orange and gold.

To be worn with them were display after display of *obi*, the wide belts wrapped around the waist. Some were even more elaborate in design than the *kimono*.

We later found out the prices of the *kimono* started at about $3,000 and could go up to $300,000. The *obi* were nearly as much—between $1,000 and $100,000.

Since we had arrived early, one of the vendors gestured to indicate she would like me to try one on. I was anxious to do so because I already owned a couple of the summer-weight cotton *yukata*, but had never worn a real *kimono* before.

I wasn't wearing the correct layers of undergarments (There would normally be several.), but that didn't deter her. She first wrapped the *kimono* tightly around me—crossing it left over right. (Right over left, as is normal for western women's clothing, is only used when dressing a corpse and is considered bad luck.) It was then tied at my waist with a thin piece of silk fabric. Next, the bottom of the robe was raised until it brushed the floor. When it was at the right height, it was folded up with the fold towards the top. Another thin silk tie was used to secure it in this location. One's breasts were supposed to be flattened out in this process—and they were.

Next came the *obi*. I knew there were women who specialized in the tying of these sashes. I had seen whole books and TV shows devoted to the art. There were many different ways of creating the shape in the back, and each one told something about the woman's social status or the formality of the occasion. To secure the *obi*, and add another design element, a twisted silken rope in a contrasting color was added on top. Because the *kimono* was straight and wrapped

---

[9] There are no plurals in the Japanese language, so the singular is used whether referring to one or many.

tightly, and since the *obi* was nearly a foot wide, I was forced to stand tall and take little tiny steps.

Fortunately it had been hot earlier in the day and I had worn my hair up. Exposing one's neck is appropriate when wearing *kimono*, and considered sexy.

I enjoyed the experience and posed for photos. I was also very grateful I wasn't expected to endure one as a matter of course. It was most uncomfortable!

Raouf and Antoine couldn't resist the chance to give me a bad time.

"I don't think you'll be mistaken for Japanese," Raouf teased me, shaking his head and assessing the overall effect.

"Not with that hair," Antoine added making reference to my reddish tresses.

"Even if you ever actually learn the language, you're never going to melt into the crowd," Raouf added. "Might as well accept it. You're a *gaijin* (foreigner) and always will be. You make a really strange looking Japanese."

They laughed. I laughed. Larry laughed. Even the *kimono* vendors laughed—and they didn't understand the conversation.

Antoine and Raouf were both artists themselves, so thoroughly appreciated the sheer beauty and creativity in the designs and patterns displayed.

I changed out of the *kimono,* and we enjoyed the show together.

*   *   *   *   *

When they made the decision to move to *Osaka*, Raouf and Antoine opted to order furniture through a Japanese catalogue provided by the company Universal had hired for this service. The furniture looked lovely in the photos and seemed like a good choice.

On the day their order was delivered to their apartment, however, Raouf received an urgent call at the office.

"Get home right now! This just isn't going to work!" Antoine loudly insisted.

The Universal relocation team contacted the furniture providers, and Raouf rushed home to see what the problem was.

What neither they nor any of the American team realized earlier was, while Japanese furniture was beautifully styled, it was actually about two-thirds to three-quarters the size of its western counterparts. A picture taken that day became famous around the office. It showed Antoine (who was about 6'4") standing next to the Japanese sofa. The seat hit him about mid-calf and the top of the back was mid-thigh. It looked like it belonged in a dollhouse. Since Raouf was also tall, there was no possibility the two of them could have sat together on the couch.

The bed was also too short. So were the dining chairs.

Fortunately they had brought some folding beach chairs from California to use outside on their roof deck, so at least they had something to sit on. Those were the only things in their apartment large enough.

After lengthy discussion and a great deal of effort on their part, the furniture people were finally able to locate a larger sofa and bed for them. But it was an important lesson for the team members yet to come.

*   *   *   *   *

On September 15, *Respect for the Aged Day*, we hosted the first of many parties at our place, and Antoine and Raouf attended. A couple of others had relocated by then, and there were more people in town on business trips, so a couple dozen people inaugurated the "party house."

A week or so later, we were invited for our first pizza party in Japan at their home. It was there where we were introduced to "American" pizza—complete with corn and mayonnaise. All pizza we were to encounter in Japan had corn on it. Most were drizzled with mayonnaise. In addition, the toppings we saw most frequently were seafood and seaweed. (A year after the opening of the park, a poll was taken of the favorite food item served in the restaurants. The winner was the tuna and mayonnaise pizza.)

We relaxed on their upstairs patio, watched the sunset and enjoyed the early fall evening. By this time we were getting to know each other very well.

We discovered that all of us (well, except Larry maybe) enjoyed bargain hunting. And the best places for great finds were the temple sales. Several of the temples in the *Osaka* area hosted these events, which were a lot like our multi-family garage sales in California. On the right day, great treasures could be unearthed. Most of the vendors were Japanese. Most of the shoppers were *gaijin*.

The temple down the hill from our church held their sale on the third Sunday of each month. So on the appointed date in October, we met Antoine and Raouf and attended services together. Then we went to the sale. That day I discovered inexpensive used *obi* for about ¥1000 each. Raouf got a yellow printed silk vest in his size. But I found the prize of the day when I bought a *haori* for ¥2000. We were each so proud of our purchases!

*   *   *   *   *

Knowing once we moved to our site offices in January of 1999 the workload would escalate dramatically, Raouf decided to take his accrued vacation and spend some time in Hawaii. At the beginning of November of 1998, he and Antoine left *Osaka* for a much-needed rest.

They arrived back looking tanned and refreshed, and were ready to get on with the building of the park. However, Raouf mentioned his stomach was bothering him a bit. When I asked him about it, he answered, "I think I ate too much rich food and fresh fruit on vacation."

After a week or so, he wasn't getting any better treating it himself with antacids. One of the relocation coordinators' personal physicians had offices in the WTC, so she made Raouf an appointment and accompanied him to act as translator.

The doctor gave him several powders and potions. (Doctors in Japan never told any of us exactly what we were getting.) He was instructed to return in a week, and he did. This continued for several more weeks with new medications each time.

*   *   *   *   *

On the 22nd of December the entire WTC office was packed up and shut down for the move to the job site. We were free until the 6th of January when, following the New Year holiday, we would move into our construction offices at the site. By then Raouf hadn't improved and had switched to another doctor.

Larry and I decided to use the time to take a much-needed trip back to California to see our families and celebrate the holidays. My mother had broken her hip in October and, although we were assured everything had healed well, she was okay, and there was no need for either of us to return immediately, I needed the reassurance of seeing her for myself.

Fortunately by the time we arrived in California, Mom was back on her feet and had made a complete recovery. After a delightful trip home, we returned to *Osaka* and the new site office.

*   *   *   *   *

In the location where a little over two years hence a world class theme park would stand, all we saw the first day were mounds of dirt, four prefabricated buildings and a small guard shack, all surrounded by a high privacy fence.

The first morning back to work began with our staff meeting. We were distressed to hear that while we were away, Raouf had gone to a third doctor with the same results: he was now in far worse pain and none of the treatment had helped. He had finally persuaded Universal to fly him back to California for definitive tests and treatment.

Later in the morning, I spotted Raouf walking past my office window. I ran out and caught him.

"You're not getting out of here without a great big hug!" I announced.

He chuckled, and then collected it. "Thanks for stopping me. I'm on my way to the airport right now."

"I'll be praying for you," I assured him.

"Thanks, I'll need it," he said. With a wave, he rounded the corner of the building and was gone. I returned to my office and he to California.

*   *   *   *   *

Larry and I attempted to stay in touch with Raouf via email and with Antoine on the phone. Raouf was not improving, yet, his emails were upbeat and he kept saying he was looking forward to getting back.

Because of an administrative oversight, there was a problem with my work visa, so I left the office a week later to wait for a corrected one. While I was at home, I invited Mrs. K., the furniture lady, for lunch. That morning I called her to find out when she would be arriving only to discover she had just left Antoine's place after helping him pack his belongings to return to California.

"What do you mean, he's packing?" I asked.

"Haven't you heard? Raouf finally has a diagnosis—it's terminal cancer. Antoine and *Kobe* will be leaving on tomorrow's flight to L.A."

I immediately called Larry to find out if they had been told. They hadn't, even though management had been informed the day before.

"Some of the guys could go over right now to help Antoine with the packing," Larry offered. "Let us know if he needs anything. We'll be waiting."

But when I called Antoine, he said, "The truck with the furniture and our personal possessions is already gone. *Kobe* and I are about to leave."

"Do you need a place to stay?" I asked? "You know we have lots of room."

"No, thanks, I've made arrangements to stay with other friends tonight and they can drive us to the airport tomorrow."

I called Larry back to update him. The *Osaka* team was devastated. Unfortunately, we were never officially informed by the company. (This may have been due more to the Japanese custom of not revealing bad news directly than to a deliberate attempt to keep us in the dark.) Universal sent a grief counselor to *Osaka*, but not until several weeks later.

*   *   *   *   *

In mid-February, my mother was again hospitalized. This time, the doctors thought perhaps she had suffered a stroke, and I was advised to return home. So I left *Osaka* for California.

Raouf and I played phone tag, but I was never able to contact or see him in person. Still, I let him know he was missed in Japan, and everyone was thinking about him.

Fortunately Mom's problem was corrected with medication, and she was released from the hospital the day after I arrived. Shortly after my return to *Osaka*, my visa problem was ironed out and I returned to the office. Frequent emails were exchanged between our group in *Osaka* and Raouf. He remained optimistic.

*　　*　　*　　*　　*

There was a tradition in Japan of folding *origami* cranes. For special occasions like weddings, a thousand cranes would be folded for good luck. And in the case of serious illness, doing the same was believed to make the ill person well. One of the team members suggested we fold a thousand cranes for Raouf. Everyone on the project—translators, engineers, art directors, managers, Japanese and American—made cranes. Each lunch hour found a group in the cafeteria with stacks of *origami* paper, creasing together.

At last we completed all the tiny cranes. Most were imperfect but all were made with love. They were strung together with thread until they resembled the branch of a willow tree, then carefully packed and sent to Raouf with our prayers and best wishes. He let us know how touched he was, and said he hung them where he could watch them swaying in the breeze.

*　　*　　*　　*　　*

One morning in April, we received an email message first thing after arriving in the office informing us of a mandatory meeting at 9:00 a.m. There was grumbling about canceling and postponing other commitments, but the team assembled as ordered.

The director of accounting & HR tearfully told us our friend Raouf had passed away in the early hours of the morning. He died peacefully, surrounded by friends and family.

Some wept; some were silent; some cursed. All were stunned. Even our Japanese translators gave in to public weeping, not acceptable under normal circumstances. But unlike our earlier experience, at least we could share our grief.

For Raouf's memorial service in California, Area 2 prepared a short video featuring clips from the farewell party held before he left for Japan. A copy of the tape was sent to us in *Osaka*, and we watched it together. There he was as we remembered him—laughing and joking and having a great time.

*   *   *   *   *

There is a tradition in theme parks of placing the names of those involved in its creation in visible locations. This is usually in the form of a name painted on an upstairs window, or a sign on a building. We were concerned that Raouf's name be appropriately displayed.

Shortly before park completion, we were finally able to locate all the team names, and discovered Raouf's special place there. In the New York area on Park Avenue is a three-story brownstone. There are steps leading up to a door-way. On the front of the building, to the left of the entrance is a cast brass plaque with the words, "Iskander Apartments". Raouf now has a permanent place in Universal Studios Japan—and in our hearts and memories as well.

The Best April Fools' Day Joke—Ever

Embed
A noun describing an insert used to affix something perma-nently to a surrounding mass.

＊   ＊   ＊   ＊   ＊

Larry

By the spring of 1999, most of the job site was still dirt. Foundations were started for some of the larger buildings, and excavation was well underway for the various park lagoons.

Until this time we had been working on paper. Changes and revisions to drawings were easily made with relatively little construction cost or schedule impact. Then we hit our first major field construction problem.

Pits built to accommodate the animated figures (sharks and dinosaurs) within the lagoons were the first to be formed and have concrete poured. Steel plates were embedded in the floor of the pits to secure the frames for the fig-ures which were to arrive later. After pouring concrete in the first seven shark pits, we noticed that these steel embedment plates were beginning to rust. In the translation of US ASTM[10] standards to the Japanese standards for steel quality, something had been lost. The contractor had used regular mild steel (carbon steel which rusts) rather than the specified stainless steel for the plates. The mild steel would not hold up in the underwater environment. What were we to do?

The animated equipment supplier along with the Hollywood Universal ride engineers and area director were flown to *Osaka*. Meetings were held, options offered, fingers pointed, costs and schedule impact to repair the problem esti-mated. There was no easy fix. The proposed solution would be expensive: jack-hammer out the concrete, replace the plates, form and re-pour the pits.

---

[10] American Society for Testing and Materials

After two weeks of intense negotiations between Universal and the GCs, the Hollywood team returned home without an agreement. The situation was tense.

*   *   *   *   *

March 31st

The *Osaka* field team (Stresh and I) was still looking for other alternatives. Late in the afternoon, I was sitting in my cubicle in the field office after yet another indecisive meeting, when Stresh walked in.

"Too bad", he mused, "we couldn't just put a stainless steel plating on those embeds, like they chrome plate auto bumpers."

"Yah, too bad," I agreed.

"Better yet, it would be nice to be able to do the plating in the field without having to remove anything."

"It would certainly be convenient and much less expensive," I added, beginning to catch on to where this conversation was going.

"Say, you have a dictionary of technical terms around, don't you?"

"Yes, it's right here on the shelf behind my desk."

Thus the germ of the project's best April Fools' Day joke was born.

Of course, no method to plate stainless steel onto regular steel existed, much less in a field application. But, with the help of some well-chosen words plucked from my faithful *McGraw-Hill Dictionary of Scientific and Technical Terms—Second Edition*, a method was "invented."

The resulting email stated the Japanese contractor had proposed this "new" method to solve our problem, and the project directors had agreed to the proposal. To keep USJ to the original schedule, it said the contractor would be starting the construction change on April 1st. The email was crafted so the first part seemed logical, the second part stretched credibility, and the final sentence was to give away the joke. Or so we thought.

————Original Message————
From: Stresh
Sent: Thursday, April 01, 1999 12:48 AM
To: Stephen [Area 3 *JAWS* technical ride engineer]
Cc: Fraser [Area 3 *Jurassic Park* technical ride engineer]; Mike [Area 3 area director]
Subject: *JAWS* Embeds

Stephen,

At the end of the day yesterday S-san [USJ Co. project director] met with D [Universal project director] and they worked out a solution for the embeds that Takenaka will start installing tomorrow.

In talking with Sumitomo Metals, Takenaka has discovered that it is possible to add a stainless steel coating to the embed plates. Sumitomo has developed a process that first nickel plates the mild steel. The plating uses nickel-molybdenum coating that is electrolytically applied. Once the nickel-molybdenum coating is hardened, then the item is ready for the stainless steel coating. The stainless steel coating is applied in a similar method but is done in an acetone bath to assure complete bonding.

They have given us a schedule to do this and will have all of the embeds plated in a week and a half. The cost per plate is approx. ¥35,000 and Sumitomo will warranty the plates for 20 years.

The only catch is that to be able to maintain this warranty, a 78 year old Shinto priest needs to bless the installation on April 1st of every leap year.

Stresh

That evening the email was sent. Since *Osaka* is seventeen hours ahead of California, it was timed to arrive in Hollywood first thing in the morning on their April 1st.

*   *   *   *   *

April 2nd, Osaka Time

When the *Osaka* team returned to work the following morning (3:30 p.m. April 1st Hollywood time), a flurry of messages, forwards and replies had crossed the world many times.

The Area 3 director, Mike, was on an inspection trip to the Midwest and checked email from his hotel room late at night. Working alone in his room, without the benefit of contact with anyone else, he read only the first part and sent emergency messages to his entire technical staff.

————Original Message————

From: Mike
Sent: Thursday, April 01, 1999 6:33 PM
To: Stresh; Larry; [Hollywood Purchasing Manager]; [Universal Project Director]
Cc: Fraser; Stephen
Subject: RE: *JAWS* Embeds
Importance: High

Just for everyone's information, you cannot weld onto a plated structure, therefore the plating must be removed prior to welding or we have to pay our vendor to change their attachment methodology. Has Sumitomo provided documentation that shows that this plating can be welded to? This is a decision that the technical team should have been consulted on. In regards to the cost, is USJ Co. asking for MORE money? Who agreed to this? We already are in the process of paying for stainless, do we get to deduct the price difference between the stainless and the mild steel, then add back on the price of the coating?

Mike

    *   *   *   *   *

Stephen, who was working in Hollywood, read the email, saw the joke, and replied to all with a similarly inventive method to avoid the plating altogether.

————Original Message————

From: Stephen
Sent: Friday, April 02, 1999 7:27 AM
To: Stresh; Larry; [Hollywood Purchasing Manager]; [Universal Project Director]: Mike
Cc: Fraser
Subject: RE: *JAWS* Embeds

Stresh,
Just recently we have heard of a new technology here in the states called "transmutation." We feel this new technology will work even better than the plating method you proposed and at lower cost.

Basically, you resonate the material at a very high frequency which matches the resonation frequency of the atomic nuclei of the material you are using.

By doing this, the amplitude of the vibration becomes so high in the nucleus that it overcomes the weak nuclear force, but the strong nuclear force remains. At this point it is possible to introduce new protons and neutrons into the nucleus. This can be done by adding heavy water (deuterium) in a plasma state to the material. The deuterium, with its extra neutrons in the plasma state, is readily absorbed into the atomic nuclei. Depending on how much deuterium you add, you can change the existing material into a completely different type of material up to two millimeters in thickness from the surface (for steel). To change the material to a lighter metal, you simply resonate the material in a complete vacuum at these special frequencies. Different atomic natural frequencies will allow transmutation into different types of materials up and down the periodic table.

The process can be done for approximately one hundred dollars per plate in a matter of days, and no blessing is required. We can basically turn these suckers into chrome.

Let us know what you think.

Stephen

Someone else suggested Teflon coating the plates to eliminate corrosion. Several more equally preposterous schemes were put forward by various other technical team members. Of course, each of these suggestions was faithfully copied to everyone involved.

For a day or so Stresh and I were not at all positive we still had jobs, but the team, including Mike, had appreciated the joke, and it seemed to help us all re-think our priorities. This problem, after all, was not the end of the world, only another challenge to overcome.

In the end, the plates were replaced, the schedule kept and construction moved forward.

*   *   *   *   *

A year later, when Stresh was leaving the project to return to the US, about sixty of the *Osaka* team, both from Universal and *Takenaka*, attended a farewell party at a local restaurant to say goodbye. During the requisite after dinner speeches (now that we were familiar with Japanese protocol), the April Fools' Day joke was acclaimed as one of the high points of the first year's activities.

The Speech

Omiage (Oh-mee-ah-geh)
Gift. The presentation of gifts is a ritual in Japan. They are given
for all occasions, and sometimes for no occasion. Attempting to
learn all the routines and requirements surrounding Japanese
gift giving was daunting.

*   *   *   *   *

Larry

Each month the general contractors (GCs) on the Universal jobsite held a progress meeting. It was a kind of rally for the workers. At these events, pep talks were made by management to inspire the troops, and recognition awards were presented for safety and/or performance on the project. The day before one of these affairs, my boss asked if I could give a short speech as the representative from USI (the Universal Studios International group based in Hollywood). Knowing I could not get out of it, I penned a few brief ideas. I thought it might be a good idea to try presenting a portion in Japanese as no one from USI had ever attempted that. So I wrote out the first part in my own system of phonetic Japanese. Then I took it to the head translation contractor, who by this time was also a friend, for his assistance in polishing it up. He made a suggestion or two, but mostly he was complimentary and enthusiastic about my attempt. I rehearsed it with him several times to make sure it sounded okay.

At 8:00 a.m. sharp on a frosty April 1st of 1999, some four hundred Japanese workers and two *gaijin* (foreigners), of which I was one, were assembled, standing in long rows in the parking area, all in work uniforms, hardhats, gloves, etc. After fifteen minutes of warm-up exercises to music and instructions—"*ichi, ni, san, yon*" (1, 2, 3, 4)—on the loudspeaker system, the construction manager welcomed everyone.

Several awards (inscribed plaques, pins, etc.) were given, both to individuals and teams, with much fanfare, formal bowing and applause. Then various Japanese facility managers and craft supervisors were called to the podium for status reports and short talks.

The addresses all tended to follow the same format: praising the workers for their performance and safety record, admonishing them to continue to perform without injury and encouraging them to keep up the good work.

Then it was my turn. I spoke, and the interpreter translated. (I must apologize to all my Japanese friends for my attempt to convert the Japanese words to English.)

*   *   *   *   *

Stepping to the podium and after the respectful bow to the group, I began.

"*Ohayo gozaimasu.* (Good morning.) *Watashi-wa Unibasaru Sutajio-no Projecto Enjinia* Larry Collins *desu.* (I am Larry Collins, project engineer for Universal Studios.) *Watashi-wa sukoshi Nihongo-ga hanashimasu, demo mada jozu jarimasen.* (I speak a little Japanese, but I am not very good yet.) *Deskara, watashi-wa Eigo-de hanashimasu.* (Therefore, regrettably, I will speak in English.)

"Universal Studios Japan began several years ago as a dream, an idea, a sketch on paper. My family moved to *Osaka* last August to be a part of the construction team and help bring this vision to life.

"Through your efforts, we are now starting to see the dream becoming a reality: a place where Universal guests can encounter a dinosaur, escape from a giant shark, ride a coaster with Snoopy, walk western streets with cowboys, see spectacular stunts and shows, and be entertained by amazing animal actors.

"I look forward to the safe and successful completion of the construction.

"I am pleased to be a member of the team that will bring the excitement, adventure and fun of this theme park to families, their children, grandchildren and beyond."

*   *   *   *   *

Since many of the workers had never seen or personally experienced the rides and attractions they were helping to build, they listened intently; and my effort was well-received.

There followed the reciting of the safety slogans by everyone and a final closing statement by the construction manager. An *omiage* (gift) of a small hand towel and a nifty ballpoint pen with four colors of ink was given to everyone who attended.

Following the meeting, I was asked by the *Takenaka* construction manager, *Hirose-san,* to join the other managers and craft supervisors in their monthly visit to pray at the local Shinto shrine. I felt privileged to be invited, as I was the first (and to my knowledge the only) American ever to be so honored.

Riding with *Hirose-san* on the way to the shrine, I was worried as I was not familiar with Shinto rituals and didn't want to unknowingly offend anyone. He must have sensed my uneasiness as he confided, "Just stick by me, follow what I do, and you will be all right."

The shrine was located only a few blocks from the jobsite and the GCs had been instrumental in restoring and repairing the roof structure, perhaps to appease the gods and bring good fortune to the project. Or maybe it was to pacify local residents who were not delighted with all the construction activity and its associated noise and dust. Either way, contented gods and a little prayer are always good things.

Arriving outside the shrine, we first proceeded to a covered area where a small fountain continuously filled a raised wooden trough about twelve feet long by two feet wide. Here we performed the ritual cleansing (hand washing) using the bamboo ladles placed on a rack over the wooden pool provided for that purpose. Then we passed through the distinctive "bird perch" *tori* (gate) into the shrine area proper. "Clap only twice," *Hirose-san* whispered as we approached the shrine itself. Each person, in turn, made an offering (a few coins from our pockets tossed through a wooden grate into a container), clapped hands (twice only) and made a silent prayer for safety on the job.

Then we all retired to the coffeehouse across the street where I was formally introduced to several construction foremen I had not met before. We performed the requisite *meishi* (business card) exchange with bows all around, and shared coffee and hard-boiled eggs before returning to work.

Altogether, it was a most memorable morning, and one I will treasure forever.

*   *   *   *   *

When I was speaking about families enjoying the park for generations to come, I was actually expressing a personal wish.

One of our Japanese "daughters," *Yasuko*, had been married several years earlier and had a two-year-old son at the time we moved to Japan. She and her family met us for dinner the first night Lorna arrived for our apartment hunting trip in May of 1998. *Daisuke* (called "*Dai-chan*") had obviously never seen foreigners before. At first he was very shy, hiding behind either his mother or his father. However, by the end of the evening, his American "Grandma" (*Obachan*) and "Grandpa" (*Ojiichan*) were carrying him around.

Yasuko and her family lived in *Osaka* and were frequent visitors. *Dai-chan* loved trains and spent countless hours on our balcony with one of the adults, peering down through the Plexiglas barriers watching the trains below as they entered and exited the stations. "*Densha, densha!* (Train, train!)," he would squeal as he pointed to the cars moving along the tracks. Since there were two stations in *Takarazuka*, the JR and the *Hankyu*, railroad traffic arrived and departed frequently.

One of the perks of my working in Hollywood for the first year was being able to take advantage of the special employee sales. They never seemed to be announced ahead of time, but word blew through the office like a hurricane, "There's a big sale on Soundstage 22 starting at 9:00 today." Or, "I just heard they're selling posters on the 9th floor. Let's go."

The items were usually the remnants of clothing styles being discontinued in the studio stores, the last of a certain movie-themed toy, overstocks that didn't sell well or closeouts with only a few pieces remaining. Our friend Pat once scored a cool *Jurassic Park* watch for me for $5.00. And I was able to get logo clothing and gifts (*omiage*) to take to Japan.

One of these sales was of artwork—originals and prints. Since I would be working on the *Jurassic Park* attraction for the next few years, I couldn't resist a set of the original concept sketches of the dinosaurs, intending to use them to decorate my workspace in Japan.

At the same sale were original hand-painted animation cels[11] from the Universal cartoon *The Little Engine That Could*. They were cute and colorful and they, too, were on sale. I phoned Lorna to ask her if she thought we should buy one. Even though we didn't need one, I kept thinking about them. Lorna felt we should get one too, just because. So I returned and spent a lot of time deciding on exactly the right cel.

There were so many to choose from, it was difficult making a selection. Quite a few had close-ups of the animal characters. But, since I hadn't seen the cartoon, I wasn't aware of which were most important.

I finally settled on a scene showing the entire train filled with colorful animals exiting a tunnel. And it came with a background and certification. The tracking holes were on the cel to prove it had been used in making the cartoon. I brought it home and put it away for some later use, whenever that might be.

---

[11] "Cel" is short for celluloid, the thin, transparent, hand painted sheets from which cartoons are created. Tracking holes are used to properly align the cels for filming.

Once we learned about *Dai-chan's* obsession with trains, however, we knew right where the cel belonged. When we returned to California for Christmas of 1998, we located the artwork and brought it back to *Osaka* with us as *Dai-chan's* birthday present. His mother was delighted and promised to have his special gift framed for his room. We also purchased a videotape of the cartoon as his Christmas gift.

We had our vast film collection with us in Japan, including over one hundred children's videos. Whenever *Dai-chan* came for a visit, he was allowed to borrow a couple to take home with him. He always wanted to take our copy of *The Little Engine That Could*, and his mother always reminded him he already had his own at home.

At the end of 1999, *Yasuko* gave birth to a second son, *Yusuke* (or *Yu-chan*). We now had two Japanese grandchildren. We continued to see them as often as possible. And we loved watching "our boys" growing up.

Each time we returned to the US on home leave, we brought back *omiage* for the boys, to their delight. We enjoyed spoiling them.

One of our last outings before leaving Japan was an afternoon visit to their new home in *Nishinomiya*, about twelve kilometers south of *Takarazuka*.

After our return to California, we received photos of *Dai-chan's* first day at school. In the picture, he is dressed in his navy short pants and Eton jacket with white collar, wearing a typical schoolboy hat.

The parents continue to send us snapshots and the annual New Year formal portraits.

So, that day in April, 1999, as I spoke of people enjoying the theme park through the generations, I was specifically thinking of *Yasuko* and her family.

When things would become overwhelmingly discouraging, or frustrating, we sometimes asked ourselves why we remained in Japan. Then we would think of our "kids," and their kids, and their grandkids. And we would remind ourselves that a major reason we wanted to create this wonderful place was so they could come, generation after generation, and tell their children and their friends, "Our American grandparents helped build this place."

Sakura

Sakura (saw-koo-rah)
Cherry Blossoms. Appreciated in Japan as the first sign of spring
with "Hanami" or Cherry Blossom viewing.

*   *   *   *   *

Lorna

In the US, I was used to starting relationships while standing in line at the supermarket. Larry has said I collect people the way others collect postage stamps. Before we moved, my Japanese friend Kay warned me not to expect to make friends easily or quickly. We, as *gaijin,* or foreigners, were unlikely to be considered friends by the Japanese.

The day we looked at our apartment for the first time, we stopped by a little hamburger place called *Burger City* in the strip mall below our new building to pick up some food to eat on the way to the airport. We went in with our relocation coordinator to order the meal. The couple behind the counter was very polite and anxious to help us. However, when they were told we would soon be moving into the building at the top of the hill, we were suddenly treated like royalty.

We had to sit down and enjoy a cup of tea while waiting for our lunch to be prepared. "Papa" spoke a little English. "My wife is studying English. She is a beginner."

"After we move in, I can help her with her English and she can help me with my Japanese," I offered, and our relocation coordinator translated.

We all smiled and bowed, happily agreeing to the plan.

As promised, I began spending time at the burger shop in the afternoons when there was a lull in business. *Misayo-san* (the wife) and I would spend hours—me with my English-Japanese dictionary and *Misayo-san* with her Japanese-English one. I began to call our exchange "dueling dictionaries." But somehow we were able to communicate.

Inability to convey ideas became a shared source of laughter. And occasionally "Papa" would attempt to fill in the blanks—resulting in more amusement.

One day shortly after our arrival, I rushed back to the apartment to breathlessly tell Larry, "Today I learned the couple at *Burger City, Misayo-san and Akira-san,* have a 22-year-old daughter, *Kazue,* who is a concert pianist. She's studying in *Kyoto* but comes home on weekends." I continued for a while with more details about the family.

Larry, who had observed the process of our "conversations," finally asked, "How on earth did you learn all that?" Neither *Misayo-san* nor I could have answered his question, but somehow we found out a great deal about each other.

During the following months, I began thinking of *Misayo-san* as my friend but assumed the sense of friendship was only on my part. Then one day while I was visiting the shop, a man entered who spoke some English. *Misayo-san* introduced him to me as a college professor who had previously lived in the area and had come to visit his family. Then she introduced me to the professor. I still understood little of the language, but had learned enough to recognize the words *"saiko tomadachi"* (best friend) in the introduction. I was nearly moved to tears when I realized that *Misayo-san* considered me not just a friend, but a best friend.

*   *   *   *   *

In April of 1999, our daughter and my mother were scheduled to arrive for a visit. When *Misayo-san* heard Mom and Kim would be coming, she immediately insisted all of us would come for dinner at her home.

We had a party their first weekend in town to celebrate Larry's birthday. Some of our Universal friends and several of our Japanese "daughters" came as well as *Misayo-san* and *Kazue.* During the evening, Mom and Kim were formally invited for dinner.

In Japan, cherry blossom viewing was a ritualized event. During a specific week, everyone in the country went to their local park or along the river or to wherever there was an abundance of trees, took a picnic, and viewed the blossoms. We joked that, for many young people, it had become a great excuse for drinking beer and getting rowdy.

Misayo-san had a pretty tree in her back yard. When it was in bloom, she trained a spotlight on it at night so it could be enjoyed from the dining area.

We were treated to a wonderful *sukiyaki* dinner. (This was to become Mom's favorite meal during her trip.) The *sukiyaki* was cooked at the table, so there was conversation and laughter during the meal. *Kazue* was home from *Kyoto* that evening to translate for us.

After dinner, the lights were dimmed, and we viewed the lighted tree while sipping homemade *sakura* wine and listening to *Kazue* play a Fantasia on "Sakura." She found out Mom had been a piano teacher earlier in her life. My mother was immediately elevated to the status of "*sensei*" or teacher.

We encouraged *Kazue* to play another selection. When she began, both Mom and I started to cry. She had chosen "Rustle of Spring." This was a favorite selection of Mom's during my childhood. It was particularly poignant since by then my mother was no longer able to play the instrument. When *Kazue* learned the piece was special to her, it became "Vera's Song" in my mother's honor. (*Kazue* came for a visit to California in the summer of 2001 and played several concerts. She ended each one with "Vera's Song.")

As we sat in the home of our Japanese friends enjoying their hospitality, good food, wonderful music and the view of the lovely delicate blossoms, I think our appreciation for this particular Japanese tradition increased dramatically.

*   *   *   *   *

Misayo-san gave me a gift for my birthday the following August—a set of fragile porcelain teacups around the rims of which were painted delicate cherry blossoms. I told her whenever we used them, Larry and I would remember our first *hanami* in Japan in the *Igo* home and the special friendship we shared.

We do.

Photo by Dave Froelich
"Hanabi Taikai" Fireworks Party 1999

Photo by Armen Kevorkian
Fireworks Party II 2000

Photo Lorna Collins
USJ Co. party for the Nihon Cowboy Fall 1998.
Jurassic Jack is just left of center on the black shirt.

Photo Yomiyuri Shinbun
This photo of the *JP* team was on the cover of the
Yomiyuri Shinbun newspaper on June 29, 2000

Photos Lorna & Larry K. Collins
Jurassic Jack's adventures. Top: Visiting Miyajima Island,
Center: Testing the boat and the rockwork for *Jurassic Park*,
Bottom: *Omiai* with Junko

Photo by Michael Hopewell

Universal Studios Japan® spring 2001.

The Ferris wheel in the background is near the museum where Groundbreaking was held.
The *Osaka* World Trade Center is the tall building in the upper right.
The *WaterWorld* arena is in the lower right corner, *JAWS* in the lower left, *Jurassic Park* in the center right and the Main Lagoon in the center left.

Larry's Vehicle

Shaken (Shaw-ken)
Japanese car registration. Cars must be inspected every three years and every year after the car is over ten years old. The inspection costs $600—$1,800.

*   *   *   *   *

Larry

Part of our relocation package was to have included the lease or purchase of an automobile while in Japan. Back in California, we had placed one vehicle in storage and sold Lorna's convertible and my surf van.

However, at the time we arrived in Japan, the Universal vehicle policy was not yet completed, and no one knew for sure when it would be. Since I was the farthest away from the office (not in kilometers, but in travel time), the company allowed me to use the rental car assigned to the relocation group until a policy was in place. We all assumed this would be for a matter of a few days, not the months it actually took.

Other expats began arriving and found housing. Most were in the *Kobe, Rokko* Island and *Ashiya* areas adjacent to major train lines. They caught the JR train east into *Osaka* (*Umeda* station) where they would change trains for the *Osaka* Loop Line headed southwest to *Bentencho* station. There they would get on the subway west to Cosmo Square and walk the two blocks to the *Osaka* WTC building. The trip averaged about two hours.

My path, heading south from *Takarazuka*, crossed the East-West JR rail line. I began stopping at the *Koshienguchi* Station in *Nishinomiya* to pick up the others, saving them about an hour's travel. My trip still took two hours to cover the twenty-six miles, but at least I now had company for the last half hour.

The *Koshienguchi* Station was tucked into a traditional Japanese suburb of narrow streets, close-set houses and shops. Finding its location the first time was a real adventure since most of the streets were one-way only. I could find no signs (in English) showing directions, so I just kept crossing back and forth under the elevated track until the station appeared. Since the train track was raised through the area, the structure itself was on two levels. The upper one was for loading and unloading, while the lower, beneath the tracks, contained ticketing, lockers and what seemed like a hundred vending machines dispensing beverages (hot and cold, alcoholic and non), smokes, magazines, etc. Passengers climbed a steep flight of stairs to the train level. The Japanese plan to make train stations handicapped accessible had not yet reached *Koshienguchi* Station.

I customarily arrived several minutes early and paused in the station's small passenger pick-up area with room for about eight cars. There were usually several waiting taxis—and me. Since most people in this area walked or rode bicycles to the station, the cycle storage lot was twice the size of the small car area and was always completely filled by the time I arrived. More parked bicycles flooded onto the streets leaving just enough room for a car to squeeze through.

Diagonally across from the station entrance ran a partially covered shopping street lined with little stores. Produce stands, a fish market, a bakery, *Mr. Donut, KFC Fried Chicken* and *Mo's Burgers* all huddled closely around the station.

From my parked car, I could get a real feel of the Japanese morning world passing by. I was enveloped in the high-pitched squeal of bicycle brakes as riders raced to find parking spaces in the overcrowded lot. I was awed by the *salarymen* in their dark business suits carrying umbrellas and zipping in and out. (How they could ride in the rain while holding open umbrellas and still control their bikes in traffic, I'll never understand.) Old men in *yukata* (summer *kimono*) smoked, drank tea and gossiped on the street corners. Shopkeepers swept in front of their stores preparing for the day's activity. And children, some as young as kindergarten, in groups of two or three (and often alone) headed for the station. Each group wore matching uniforms (boys in short pants, girls in skirts and "Madeline" hats) and all with matching backpacks. I couldn't picture five-year-olds back in California traveling unescorted on the train to school each day. But there, it was a natural occurrence.

Right on time, (Japanese trains were always on time.) the local from *Kobe* would arrive and the others would join me for the rest of the trip to the office.

*   *   *   *   *

Finally in April of 1999, the long-awaited automobile policy was completed and we could begin looking for our own car. Since our length of stay had been reduced to the point where a lease was no longer an option, we began to research purchasing a vehicle. In Japan, new cars were expensive, but used cars

115

were relatively inexpensive because the cost of the *shaken* (safety inspection) increased as the car aged, making older ones less desirable.

I visited several used car lots in the Kobe area and spotted a Toyota "LiteAce" van that would do nicely for work and surfing, but several items had to be in place first:

Parking

Before we could buy a car in Japan we were required to have an assigned place to park it. While looking for housing the previous May, one criterion was parking. We were assured our apartment's parking structure had a spot available. When the time came to buy our car, we had to obtain a letter from the building management (complete with a map showing our personally-designated space) certifying that we, indeed, had a location to put the vehicle.

Insurance

In order to get insurance, our employment had to be verified to the company issuing the policy—especially since the purchaser was a *gaijin*. Fortunately the relocation office had made arrangements with an auto insurance vendor to provide coverage for all of the expats if we needed it. We did. It eliminated the hassle of finding a policy on our own.

Inkan Certificate

We already knew that for major purchases or actions involving the government or banks, not only was an *inkan* (personal stamp) required, but it had to be accompanied by a certificate of authenticity. These certificates were only valid for ninety days, so a trip back to the city offices in *Takarazuka* to purchase a current certificate was necessary.

Translator

The auto salesman did not speak English. My Japanese was not up to the task. So taking a translator with us was a must.

*   *   *   *   *

Armed with the required paperwork and with a translator we hired from the office to help us, Lorna and I returned to the automobile dealership, nego-

tiated and became proud owners of a beige 1998 Toyota "LiteAce" eight passenger van. I wrote the following description in an email to our friends back
home:

> It is a 1998 Toyota LiteAce (sold only in Japan). It is between
> the sizes of the VW van and my old Ford Aerostar. We picked
> it up on Friday and it has already been modified. We have
> added racks (for surfboards, of course) and changed the old
> radio for an AM/FM cassette player. Surfing stickers and
> antenna ball will go on this week.
>
> The van is equipped with seven full-sized seats and one
> smaller jump seat. The middle row of seats can be rotated to
> face forward, backward or sideways. Six of the seats recline
> fully. There is even a hot/cold box between the front seats that
> will make ice. The van roof has no less than six tilt-up sun
> roofs. It has about 48,000 kilometers (30,000 miles) on it and
> is very clean and in good shape.

We added another 25,000 miles in the following two years while we owned
it, including several trips to *Shikoku* Island off the coast of *Kobe*. Aside from
one required repair and the cost of the required *shaken*, the van proved to be a
reliable, economical and very comfortable vehicle.

*   *   *   *   *

About a year after we purchased the van, I began to hear a "clunk" in the
steering when I made a wide right turn. Over the next week, it occurred again
several more times and appeared to be getting worse. My crawling under the
van and looking around revealed nothing: no leaks, nothing loose that I could
find. Still the "clunk" persisted.

Several kilometers from the site field office in *Sakurajima* was a gas station I
frequented regularly. Frequenting regularly meant that a relationship had been
developed, a very important requirement for all business in Japan. One of the
attendants was from Peru and spoke Spanish as well as Japanese—but little
English. We spoke English and a smattering of both Spanish and Japanese. By
judicious use of the three languages, we were able to converse about more than
just the weather. Generally, gas stations in Japan are limited to fueling, oil
changes, lubrication and tires. However, attached to this station appeared to be
an auto repair facility.

During my lunch break, I loaded my bicycle in the van (just in case I needed to leave the van and bicycle back to work) and headed for the gas station. Some tri-language discussion revealed that the actual repair facility was at another station across the street. So, after work Lorna and I drove to the second location. We attempted to explain the problem without success since we were missing our Spanish-speaking interpreter. Finally, the head mechanic came over. He drove the van and then crawled underneath and began removing parts. After about forty minutes, he put everything back and, with much apology and bowing, conveyed to me it would need to be repaired at a dealership. I thanked him (also apologizing in Japanese fashion for taking his time) and asked the price for his work. He refused any payment indicating he had not been able to fix it; therefore there would be no charge.

There was a Toyota dealership in *Takarazuka* I passed each day on my way to and from work, but it was generally closed by the time I got there in the evening. That night, returning from work, Lorna and I stopped by and pulled up to the closed door of the service department to read their hours of operation. While we were deciphering the Japanese, a salesman came out of the nearby showroom. We explained the problem with gestures, pointing and much hand waving.

The salesman called to someone in the closed repair shop who immediately came out, looked the van over, opened the main service door and wheeled the van inside. We were ushered into the showroom and offered a seat and a cup of tea. Another forty minutes passed, and then the van was returned. The mechanic apologized, explaining with the use of a diagram that the special part was needed to complete the repair. It would have to be ordered and would take two days to arrive—this conveyed by pointing to a calendar. He had, however, made a temporary repair that would last until the new part could be installed.

I made arrangements to drop off the van for repair in two days and took out my wallet. Both the salesman and mechanic waved "No, no." There would be no charge for this evening. It was long past closing and these two had stayed to assure that two unknown *gaijin* were helped. We were amazed and very grateful.

Two evenings later, the repair was completed while we ate dinner at a nearby restaurant, and the van was as good as new. Although our experience had led us to expect the work to be very expensive, the total for the part and installation was only about $250. The price was more than reasonable, and we were treated to Japanese courtesy at its best.

*   *   *   *   *

At last the time for our departure from Japan arrived. A year before, we had arranged with a US-based non-profit organization to donate the van. However, by the time we were ready to leave, the program had been stopped. We were faced with the same dilemma as all the other expats with vehicles—how to sell a used car where there was no market for them.

We spread the word among all of our friends, but the prospects for a sale grew increasingly discouraging. Many in our group simply gave their cars away before they left.

However, about a week before our departure, we received a call from the man who had previously coordinated the automobile donation program. He had been contacted by a young couple who were missionaries in Japan and had been told by the charitable organization to see if he knew of any available vehicles. Since he was aware we would be leaving shortly, he called us.

We were able to donate the van to the group, and they, in turn, would give it to the couple. We would receive a receipt from the organization making our donation tax deductible. And the couple would have a great vehicle during their time in Japan.

The weekend before we left for home, the young man, Alan, took the train to *Takarazuka* to take possession of the van. He was delighted as he drove away in our trusty transportation vehicle. And we were pleased to see our old reliable friend find a good home.

*   *   *   *   *

But that was not the end. A year later when another *shaken* was required on the van, we received an urgent email from Alan, the new owner, explaining that the van had never been transferred out of my name. It seems the paperwork from the organization making it clear the title was being transferred from me to them was in English. The title paperwork in Japanese was from the organization to the new owner. But the Japanese government failed to make the change because they did not understand the three-way transfer.

I was required to write a statement that I no longer had any interest in the van, and it now belonged to the new owner. I had this statement legally signed and notarized. And for good measure, I also stamped it with my *inkan*.

I added copies of all of the original paperwork to the statement and was ready to send the package to Japan when we discovered an old out-of-date *inkan* certificate of authenticity. I threw it in too—just in case.

A week or so later I received another email from Alan, the van's now-legal owner, thanking me for providing all the documentation. Being Japan, it turned out the only document the bureaucrats were interested in was the out-of-date *inkan* certificate. No one read English and neither my signature nor the notary was recognized as legal. But the *inkan* with its expired certificate was.

And There Were Skirmishes...

Tatemai (ta-tey-my)
To say what you think people want to hear
Honne (hoe-nay)
To speak your mind openly

*   *   *   *   *

Lorna

Doing business with the Japanese meant always being aware that the "polite" response to our associates had to be couched in *tatemai* terms. It would have been considered rude to simply speak one's mind (*honne*) in a formal meeting.

In contrast, our American team was raised to be honest and say what they meant. The Japanese formality sometimes felt like a verbal straightjacket.

Since I stored all the proprietary documentation for the project, my office was one of the few truly private places in the compound. Shortly after we moved to the site, I noticed various team members stopping by after long and difficult meetings, just to "let off steam." My role was to listen.

Although we were working pretty well with the general contractors (GCs) there were still pesky issues which cropped up. And since my office was where the frustrations were expressed, I alone heard about them. These are a few of the more memorable ones.

Kitchens

In American commercial kitchens, the large exhaust hoods over all the cooking equipment contained automatic fire systems. If something on a grille or in a fryer flamed, fire suppression would be triggered to extinguish the blaze. I knew about this because at one time I had worked for a company which provided the heating, ventilation and air conditioning for commercial restaurants.

The first drawings we received showed no fire suppression systems, automatic or manual.

Hamachan, the Food Service Manager, arrived to look over the drawings. "I can't believe they left out fire suppression. Other drawings must show it."

"No," I replied. "This is all we received."

"I need to follow up on this. These places will be open for twelve to fifteen hours a day with cooking equipment running the whole time. We can't risk not having a proper safety system."

He returned a day or two later to vent. "I asked the GC about the fire systems and was told, 'We don't do that in Japan.' When I asked what happened in case of fire, I couldn't get an answer. I assume the restaurants just burn down. And guess what else? You know the 'make-up' fans that are supposed to bring fresh air from the outside to feed the hood exhaust? They're located so far from the exhaust fans, they'll have little effect, and the fans will end up sucking expensive air-conditioned air out of the building."

Hamachan was persistent. He wanted "his" kitchens to be efficient and safe. Many meetings later, fire systems were added and the fans moved.

Toilets

This one took a long and arduous path to resolution. Originally, Tony had negotiated public restrooms in the park at 75% western-style and 25% Japanese-style, with western toilets nearest the door and Asian models further inside. This was in keeping with the intended American experience in the park.

After Tony left the project, drawings were received from the GCs showing nearly all Japanese-style toilets (porcelain-lined holes in the floor) in the public restrooms. Why? They cost less and required less space than their western counterparts. Stresh took up the cause to restore some of the western-style toilets.

For a while discussions seemed to be going well. Then one day Stresh looked dejected and I asked, "What's the matter?"

"We may have to give some on the restroom issue," he confided. "The projected park attendance has been increased again, and we'll need to squeeze more toilets into the public facilities. Those Japanese stalls are smaller than our western-style ones, so more Japanese toilets can be fitted into each space."

For several months, the configuration of the facilities underwent change on a regular basis until, in the end, the ratio ended up about 75% Japanese and 25% western, with Asian ones near the entrance and American ones toward the back.

Crooked Buildings

Even Larry occasionally showed up with a gripe. "They've done it to us again," he moaned.

"What?"

"The buildings on *JAWS* Island are supposed to be falling down, so some of them should be leaning and others should have sagging roofs. The original mark-ups to the GCs clearly showed the angle of lean and amount of sag. But the latest revisions came back with the walls vertical and the rooflines straightened again.

"We've had meetings, sent memos, held conference calls, and even sent photos of old, falling-down buildings. And they still haven't gotten it. The last time the walls were straight, but one roof had a perfect chevron (v) in the middle of it."

It took several more tries before the GC design team finally understood the concept. Then, during the construction phase, this issue arose again.

"I'm really frustrated. The construction group straightened the walls and roofs on the island. It took such a long time for the design group to get the concept. Now we have to start all over again."

More time was spent explaining, drawing and convincing before *JAWS* Island finally had its old falling-down buildings.

Speakers

Speakers were located everywhere in theme parks, although most were hidden. They were in fake "trees" and "rocks," stuck up between the plants in the landscaping, and were mounted throughout show areas.

Speakers were used for area-wide sound, parade music, show effects and ambient sounds. The audio crew worked extremely hard to be sure volume and balance were perfect. If they did their job well, guests had a great time without ever knowing. (But they might leave the park humming a tune.)

The *WaterWorld* show was staged in a huge arena. The one in Hollywood held about 2000 people. Our new one in *Osaka* would be 50% larger. This was a live stunt show featuring several actors. However, only the lead characters wore microphones and spoke during the show. All the other dialogue and sounds were pre-recorded, so the speaker system was crucial.

The original specifications called for small but very powerful state-of-the-art models. Our sound team had worked with this brand before and knew what they would produce. Unfortunately, they were not made by a Japanese manufacturer, and our agreement with the Japanese was that specifications for one product could be substituted with equivalent products made in Japan, as long as they met the same criteria.

The GC proposed alternates to the speakers. The technical requirements were the same, and our sound crew approved the substitution.

Then they arrived on site.

Audio Bob stomped into my office. "You should see the *WaterWorld* speakers. They're as big as refrigerators! If they hang from the canopy as planned, the entire upper deck won't be able to see the show."

"How could that have happened?" I asked.

"The specifications for the substitution didn't disclose the size changes. Our guys assumed they'd be the same. Now we're too far along to buy replacements, so we'll have to use these monstrosities. How the heck are we going to disguise them?"

Before a new plan could be devised, the GCs installed the enormous speakers in their planned locations, and they did block the view as feared.

The GCs wanted to leave them in place, but the art directors and show producer wouldn't allow it.

Negotiations were undertaken. The final solution was to move the speakers down to the deck, theme them as large crates and cover them with fishnet. The ambient sound was a bit compromised by this move, but the overall show was salvaged.

Boats

"We're having problems with the city of *Osaka*," the construction manager confided one day. "For *JAWS* and *Jurassic Park*, we've called our ride vehicles 'boats' even though they run on tracks and are computer controlled. Turns out, it was a big mistake.

"*Osaka* is a port city, and there are strict rules about water craft. All 'boats' here must be driven by a licensed harbor pilot and marked with a registered ID in Japanese. They say we have to follow all the navigation rules. Period.

"About two years ago, I had a series of meetings with the city and port authorities, and convinced them our 'boats' should more correctly be called 'ride vehicles' because there's no driver, and they don't really float. They agreed to license them, at an outrageous cost for the deferment, and to waive the Japanese identification.

"Now, the city has new officials; and I have to start over as if original negotiations never happened."

More painful discussions, debates, deliberations—and delays ensued. At one point it appeared neither attraction might be able to open with the park.

The situation was finally resolved to no one's total satisfaction. But the "boats" were able to be used, and the attractions opened on time.

Handicapped Access

The building codes in *Osaka* required raised dots in a particular pattern on the sidewalks along main routes with directional raised bars whenever there was an intersection or crosswalk. These dots were an unending source of annoyance on public sidewalks in the city because they presented trip hazards in good weather and slip hazards in wet weather. They were usually painted neon yellow (although, because they were for the blind, this seemed to make little sense) or were shiny chrome. In observing the public, we had noticed most people—including the blind—consciously avoided these raised areas. We all did.

At a staff meeting a year or so prior to opening, "Bowtie" Dave announced, "The city of *Osaka* is now insisting the sidewalks and walkways in the park are for public access, and they have to have the handicapped dots."

A chorus of groans and objections arose.

"Don't worry, management is arguing they're on private property and, therefore, not subject to the same requirements as public thoroughfares. We're sending the construction manager with his best Japanese manners and polite language to confront the city."

Diplomacy was undertaken, large payments were made for waivers, stamps were affixed to many documents until, at last, the city agreed the park was a private location and the dots would not be required.

Then came the new city administration who again insisted the handicapped dots were necessary.

Cambria Cat arrived in my office on a daily basis with a new bad joke about "dinosaur poop" dots in *Jurassic Park* and "horse dropping" dots on the western streets.

"They're even targeting the raised boardwalk in my western area. How are we going to theme neat rows of raised bumps on a wooden walkway? It will be hard enough to explain them on 'Rodeo Drive' or 'Hollywood Boulevard.' The clock's running, and we need to get this settled."

Thank goodness for the perseverance of the construction manager. And thank goodness for his native bargaining skill. An agreement was finally drafted and approved.

In the end, with the payment of stiff fees, apologetic bows, and officially stamped permits, the park was completed as originally intended with the loathed handicapped markers ending outside the front gates. None of us knew quite how he pulled it off. And no one cared, as long as they weren't incorporated into the design.

*   *   *   *   *

After we returned from Japan, I heard from two different people that my office was referred to as the "project confessional." It was one place where frustrated Americans could gripe without violating any of the Japanese rules of etiquette. And everything said there remained there—until now.

Holidays

Matsuri (maht-soo-ree)
Festival

*　　　*　　　*　　　*　　　*

Lorna

While we were in Japan, our office observed the Japanese holidays. However, we also tried to celebrate our own. Many Japanese ones were new to us; and our neighbor and friend *Misayo Igo* became our teacher in this regard. At the same time, she and some of our other Japanese friends and "family" were fascinated by the celebrations we were accustomed to in the US. Whenever an American holiday rolled around, we invited some of them to share it with us.

The following are samples of our experiences—Japanese and American:

*　　　*　　　*　　　*　　　*

Thanksgiving—November 25, 1998

We invited our Japanese daughter *Yuka* and her friend *Yoko* to enjoy a real American-style Thanksgiving dinner. However, actually preparing the meal was quite a challenge.

TURKEY? WHAT'S A TURKEY?

The Japanese didn't seem to eat turkey. We couldn't find any in the local markets. After asking around, we finally discovered how foreigners got them.

We could have ordered one a month or two in advance with the Foreign Buyers' Club (FBC). FBC imported products for expatriates, but orders had to be placed several weeks ahead. All turkeys arrived frozen.

Or we could have checked at the Price Club to see if any happened to show up. The Price Club bore little or no resemblance to the stores of the same name in the US. It was the size of a very small American neighborhood grocery and imported foreign goods in limited quantities. The variety changed all the time. When we saw an item we wanted, we bought it.

About six weeks before Thanksgiving, we spotted a frozen, boneless, rolled turkey there, bought it and considered ourselves fortunate to have found it.

HOW TO COOK IT?

One of the reasons we decided on the turkey roast was there were few conventional ovens in Japanese homes. Some places constructed for or by expatriates had them, but our apartment (*mansion*), built for wealthy Japanese, didn't.

When our student, *Fumiko*, first saw our kitchen in California, she pointed at our oven and asked, "What's that?"

We had a fish broiler in *Takarazuka*, though. It was about four inches wide by six inches deep. Since most of the fish we saw were very small, I guess it might have worked, but ours was still untouched when we left.

We also had a combination convection/microwave oven. It was less than one cubic foot, much smaller than the microwave we'd left in California. And it was certainly too small to cook a turkey—even a rolled one. We used the microwave all the time, but never mastered the convection part. The temperatures were in centigrade, and the manual and controls were in Japanese. (This was true for all our appliances.)

We had taken a toaster oven with us, and it was a godsend. But since I would be preparing other dishes for our holiday meal, I cooked the turkey in my crock pot. Once it was carved, the slices looked fine, and there was lots of gravy.

MASHED POTATOES

Those were a cinch. We found potatoes in the market. And, although they were quite a bit smaller than the ones available in the US and were sold in smaller quantities (two to six per bag), they boiled and mashed very well.

DRESSING? WHAT DRESSING?

Unfortunately we couldn't run to the nearest market and pick up prepared packaged mixes. And as for making dressing from scratch, the only kind of bread sold was white. Occasionally we found a variation, like egg or orange, but basically, it was a white bread nation. There was no cornbread, cornmeal or cornbread mix. A couple of weeks earlier, we had happened upon one bag of stuffing mix at the Price Club. It was about half the size of a package we'd have bought in California. But it was there. So we bought it.

The recipe called for celery. We had seen it in the stores. Occasionally. One stalk at a time. For about ¥230 ($2.00) for one stalk (not a bunch). We found some. We bought it. I used it.

CANDIED YAMS

Fortunately the stores carried delicious sweet potatoes. I'd planned on cooking those, but happened to discover the last two cans of yams at the Price Club. We put them in our basket. We didn't look at the price.

Miniature marshmallows were readily available. So we had candied yams with miniature marshmallows, a childhood comfort food.

PEAS, PLEASE

Peas are Larry's favorite vegetable, and we usually had them for Thanksgiving dinner. However, they were quite rare in Japan. Several weeks earlier we spotted some at the big *Daiei* in town, so we saved a package to serve on the holiday. When they could be found, the quantities were very small. But those lovely little green vegetables sure tasted good—and familiar.

CRANBERRY SAUCE

This was another rarity, but once again, Price Club came through with a can.

ROLLS

Like potatoes, these were available and excellent. The dinner rolls were delicious, and the croissants fabulous.

PUMPKIN PIE

At first I had thought about making Larry's family favorite: *Auntie Wanda's Pumpkin Pie*. But there were some ingredients (like molasses and condensed milk) impossible to get on short notice. I also hadn't seen any heavy whipping cream or solid shortening for a crust. Instead, I decided to make my Aunt Muriel's *Pumpkin Chiffon Pie*. I had already ordered some prepared graham cracker and shortbread crusts from FBC for just such an occasion.

129

In anticipation of the holidays, I had also ordered a case of canned pumpkin when we first arrived. I had more than enough to last throughout our stay and gave the last two cans away the week we left.

I was certain I had taken several boxes of instant vanilla pudding, necessary for this recipe, but I was in the middle of making the pies when I discovered I didn't have any. And there was no option of running to the market to get it.

So I made my favorite custard filling recipe from scratch, and added the pumpkin to that. It wasn't as firm as it should have been, but it tasted good.

DECORATION

The previous Sunday at the temple sale in *Kobe* (source of many bargains) I found an old *obi* at a good price. It was orange, peach, pink and gold. I put a white sheet on the table, then cut the *obi* and used the larger piece as a table runner and the smaller piece as an accent on the library table we used as a sideboard. It looked very elegant. (This was an old and worn *obi*. Otherwise I would never have cut it.)

THE DINNER

I actually managed to get everything on the table at the same time with the hot things hot and the cold things cold. The girls really enjoyed the experience. So did we. It was nice to be able to share this most American tradition with one of our Japanese daughters.

[*Kazue and Misayo shared the following year's Thanksgiving dinner with us. By then I had learned to plan ahead, so the preparation was much easier. That year I made Auntie Wanda's Pumpkin Pie for dessert. It was the hit of the meal.*]

* * * * *

Doll Festival—March 3, 1999

Misayo invited us to her home for a special dinner to celebrate the Doll Festival (*Hina Matsuri*) which fell on March 3rd each year.

Traditionally, when a little girl was born, her parents began a doll collection for her, with additions each year as she grew older. Few families we met had continued this custom for their daughters because the figures were very expensive. However, *Kazue* had an impressive display.

The pieces were formally arranged on a multi-tiered stair-step stand in the *tokonoma*—a special alcove area in the *tatami* room. *Kazue's* was about six feet tall and had seven shelves.

The first dolls a girl received were the Emperor and Empress. Courtiers were added next, then all kinds of accessories for their comfort. On the top tier of *Kazue's* display, along with the Emperor and Empress, were beautiful lanterns. These were electrified and had gels inside them which turned with the heat of a light bulb to create a moving stained glass effect. Between the Emperor and Empress was a *taiko* drum. All the accessories were made of black lacquer, beautifully decorated in gold, with attention to every small detail.

The second tier held three maids, each with a different accessory for the royal couple. With them were more furniture pieces (small tables, etc.).

On the third step sat two guards. One held a fan; the other was an archer with arrows and quiver. Between them stood a platform with imitation colored *mochi* or sweet pounded rice. On each side were two more warriors dressed in traditional Japanese armor.

The rest of the levels contained miniature chests, tables, chairs, dishes, a tea ceremony cabinet with all the miniature implements, and even a rickshaw. Each piece was finely crafted.

On the bottom shelf at one end was a *mikan* or mandarin orange tree. On the other side was a *sakura* or cherry tree.

Dinner was as exquisite as the dolls. It is said that in Japan the food is a feast for the eye as well as the palate. Instead of serving all the food on the same plate, several small dishes make up each place setting. And, just as with a formal western table, there is a specific place in the arrangement for all the pieces.

Misayo served us on a matched set of red and gold lacquerware plates and little dishes. There were also stemmed wine glasses and *sake* cups. The *hashi* (chopsticks) were placed in front of the diner, resting on their *hashi-oke* (chopstick rest).

Dinner was presented to us with Japanese style and elegance. *Misayo* brought to the table a large three-tiered lacquerware *bento* or lunch box. We wouldn't have mistaken this for the metal Roy Rogers or Hopalong Cassidy ones we had carried as kids. This was a real treasure and work of art. It was about nine inches square with three nesting trays and a cover.

The decorated cover was removed and the top layer contained miniature fish balls colored white, pink and green on miniature skewers. We had seen larger-sized ones at food stands near parks and shrines. There were also delicate little pockets of fried tofu, cooked balls of mashed potato, tiny slices of carrot cut into flower shapes and pieces of pumpkin (what we would call "pumpkin squash") cut into one inch high hexagon shapes. This tray was lifted off and placed on the table to reveal the second layer.

It held plain and sesame-covered rice balls (*kamaboko*) often used as decoration. They're actually made from fish—a small half circle of white with a pink edge. There were also tiny packets of scrambled egg tied with thin pieces of *nori* (seaweed). This tray was removed to reveal the bottom layer containing *o-sushi*, a bed of cooked, vinegar rice with slivers of fried egg on top.

Then *Misayo* brought a plate of chicken nuggets, another plate of small chicken pieces with a different coating and a plate of red beans. Small side dishes contained a bit of soy sauce and *wasabi* (horseradish) for dipping.

Last, she offered us covered bowls of *udon* (Japanese noodle soup).

The wine and *sake* were poured, and we enjoyed a meal that was truly a feast. Minute portions of rice and red beans were put on a miniature plate for the dolls.

For dessert we had fresh strawberries drizzled with a little sweetened milk. The dolls were offered their share as well.

The food was delicious, but the highlight of the event was our enjoyment of each other.

*   *   *   *   *

Independence Day—July 4, 2000

Our last year in Japan, we invited a large group to our home to enjoy a traditional 4th of July barbecue. Our California friends, Dave and Ruth, had just arrived for a visit, so it was also a chance to introduce them to our co-workers, friends and Japanese "family" including *Misayo-san* and *Kazue*.

The evening before, we had decorated the apartment using fans I had purchased in the US, embellished with a flag motif. With a red tablecloth and white napkins and accessories, it looked very patriotic.

While I was at work, Ruth made potato salad for the festivities. In addition, I had prepared baked beans, a green salad and brownies. We served assorted chips and other snacks, besides the customary hamburgers and hot dogs. Most of our guests brought additional snacks, sweets and desserts. We fired up the charcoal in the small barbecue we had purchased at the Price Club. Two of the Japanese guys commandeered the spatulas and became our cooks for the evening.

Many of the people who attended were Japanese and had never experienced a real "American-style" 4th of July before. We played lots of patriotic music, and ate our meal on the balcony while enjoying the twinkling lights of *Osaka* at night. We lamented the absence of fireworks, but God had other plans. He provided a fabulous thunderstorm that no man-made pyrotechnics or laser show could begin to match. And He waited until we were finished with our barbecue before it began.

Most people viewed the heavenly display from inside, but our friend Casey insisted on remaining out-of-doors where he could get the full effect of the thunder and lightning.

Everyone enjoyed the party. Dave and Ruth got to meet our friends, and we were able to introduce the Japanese to a real "red, white and blue" Independence Day celebration.

Water, Water Everywhere

Sekozu (say-koh-zoo)
Literally "Construction Drawings"
Hundreds of design drawings were produced, reviewed and revised by the Universal Hollywood team and our vendors during the design phase. Then all these drawings were re-drawn by the Japanese GCs into sekozu drawings, which were again reviewed, marked up and revised on-site during construction.

*   *   *   *   *

Larry

Three of the four major lagoons, the *Jurassic Park* and *JAWS* water rides and the *WaterWorld* show, were physically in my area of the park. Only the Main Lagoon was assigned elsewhere. So, early in the project, the lagoon water systems became my responsibility. It didn't matter that my background was in electrical engineering. As the project engineer, I was supposed to know about everything.

One of my tasks was to develop a water control and transfer scheme to handle the twenty-two million gallons used in the park's lagoons. The major source of this commodity in Japan was rainfall and snow melt, so it was scarce and expensive to buy. We needed to conserve as much as possible. Also, the chosen site location on *Sakurajima*[12] was originally a manufacturing area and had not been planned to meet the water needs of a major theme park. The city supply was severely restricted, and the existing sewer system was not adequate to accommodate heavy flood runoff. The first-time fill of the Main Lagoon took more than a month using all available resources on the island. We also needed to hold rainwater on the site and release it slowly into the city's system over several days to prevent overwhelming existing drain lines.

---

[12] Translated as "Cherry Blossom Island," although trees, if any, were scarce

It's the Pits

In both *JP* and *JAWS*, animated figures (sharks and dinosaurs) emerged from the water during the course of the adventure. While the lagoons themselves were only about three feet deep, the pits housing these creatures and associated machinery could be as much as thirty feet deep. Each night, the figures needed to be inspected, maintained and repaired should a problem be found in any of the hydraulic, electrical, sensing or mechanical systems.

It was done like this: After the guests went home, the maintenance crew raised a flexible plastic wall around each pit from below the surface. These barriers were much like above-ground swimming pool walls, except the water was held out rather than in. With the enclosure in place, the contents were drained and equipment inspected. After any necessary work was completed, the water was replaced and the flexible wall lowered back out of sight. In the case of the shark pits at *JAWS*, it meant some one million gallons had to be removed, temporarily stored and replaced each night.

But what were we to do with the extra water?

Ebb & Flow

Several schemes for water containment were considered and rejected. Finally, it was agreed to use the Main Lagoon for the excess water storage. The banks would have to be extended a full meter (a little more than three feet) above the "normal" water level to accommodate an anticipated 100-year storm and allow for the nightly transfer of water from the other lagoons during maintenance.

Functionally, this created a problem with the planned Lagoon Show featuring a central water fountain and pyrotechnic effects. The water had to be at a certain level for the fountains to operate correctly and the pockets holding pyrotechnics for the fireworks show had to be kept dry and above the water line. However, we were confident the transfer scheme would be functional and the details could be worked out later.

Falling Waters

As part of my daily noon walk in Hollywood I visited *Jurassic Park*, and my routine included reading the flow rates on the existing waterfall pumps. They averaged between 2,700 and 3,000 gallons per minute (gpm). In a money-saving effort, called Value Engineering (VE), it was suggested we purchase smaller pumps for *Osaka,* cutting the flow in half. But, the waterfall rock face at our

135

ride was twice the size of the one in Orlando and even larger than the Hollywood facility. Both the rockwork consultant and I objected to reducing the pump size. Unlike Hollywood's, our waterfall was split into two streams at the top: one side fed a 120-foot straight fall into the lagoon, while the second flow bounced, bubbled and cascaded over a bolder-strewn path to the bottom. We both felt the visual impact would be greatly reduced. To make our point, we had even begun to refer to the VE design as the "water drool."

However, money (or potential savings) talks, and we needed to convince others that the full-size fall was really needed. Finally, we swung the art director to our side and, with his help and some judicious negotiations—losing a couple of trees and reducing the complexity of some of the other rockwork—we were able to keep the full-size pumps.

Two years later when testing the falls, we were vindicated. At the upper fall, the art director even added hoses (out of guest sight, of course) to redirect water flow and make a bigger-looking splash. By then he was wishing for still more water, but at least he did not have to contend with what might have actually been a "water drool."

Crystal Clear

Once the park had the water it needed, we would have to keep and reuse as much as possible. There were also code requirements for the water quality for each attraction. This meant a treatment system.

The *WaterWorld* show would have several actors immersed repeatedly throughout the day. So swimming pool quality was needed. Ride vehicles were used in *Jurassic Park* and *JAWS*, so water was only splashed on the guests. Per the Japanese construction code, we could use a treatment level called "Dabble Water" for those attractions. And since the Main Lagoon was to share water with *JAWS* and *JP* each night, it had to be of the same quality.

Takenaka recommended using a state-of-the-art, multi-layer bio-mass system for *JP*, *JAWS* and the Main Lagoons. This process first circulated the water through gravel filters, then a crushed coral layer to regulate ph balance, then through a bio-filter where the good microbes (creepy-crawlies) ate the bad ones, then a "flocculation" process where small suspended particles were clumped together for easier removal, finally processing the water through a sand filter to remove any residue. This type of system would have been prohibitively expensive had we wanted to use it in the US parks, but a Japanese supplier provided it at substantial savings in exchange for some advertising. Still, experts from Hollywood were flown in to approve the decision since this was a change from the recommendations of the original report.

During the review, a potential problem became evident: the water would be too clear! Lagoon bottoms were crisscrossed with pipes, conduits, air-lines and signal cables. Also, circulation pumps, underwater lighting and those animated figures lurked just below the surface. Even though pipes and equipment were painted the same color as the bottom, they could still be seen through clear water. I spent several months working in a small test pond near *WaterWorld*, adding various dyes and colorings to see if these would be able to hide the underwater equipment. I also had to suspend samples of the dinosaur and shark skins to be sure they would not be affected by the dyes. After all, an ultra-saur with aqua blue legs might not look very convincing. I needn't have worried. The dyes did not hurt or discolor the skins, and the water treatment system worked so well all trace of dye was removed within forty-eight hours.

Finally, the supplier agreed to reduce the efficiency to allow for some cloudiness (officially called "turbidity") in the lagoons. Since this process was very slow to react to water quality changes (algae growth, etc.), maintaining the increased turbidity would make the system extremely difficult to control. The maintenance crew would have their hands full finding a way to balance water clarity and algae prevention. But it meant the "primeval swamp" look preferred by art direction might be achieved.

Flooding Averted

All the water requirements were included in an overall facilities report issued before I left Hollywood. Resolving the Main Lagoon issues was the responsibility of the project engineer for another area.

Then I moved to Japan.

During the following months, there were numerous changes in staff. Tony, the A&E director, left the company. Two of the five project engineers were replaced along with several of the facility design managers. Area directors departed, and those who were left were moved from their original areas to others. Attraction managers changed attractions. Some people decided not to move. During this transition period, I was trying to cover several other park areas in addition to my own. Finally, staff changes settled down and I could concentrate again on Area 3.

Construction began on the lagoon walls. *Yamaguchi-san* of USJ Co. asked me to look over the Main Lagoon *sekozu* as he had some questions, and the project engineer responsible was out of town. He remembered I had worked on the original plans in Hollywood.

When we reviewed the drawings, alarm bells rang. Portions of the Main Lagoon walls were only one foot above the water line, not the three feet needed. This meant a heavy storm or transfer water would flood some areas of the park.

Emergency meetings were called. The GCs objected as they would need to extend the walls, re-grade the area and redesign drainage around the lagoon. The GCs insisted they had not been told of the lagoon height requirements.

Since my electronic records had been destroyed in my move to Japan, I needed to find the documentation from two years before where we had informed the GCs about the water level. Fortunately, after many calls to Hollywood, another project engineer located a copy of the report letter and emailed it to me.

The letter, passed through the hands of USJ Co., convinced the GCs that the information had been available. They fixed the walls.

Going Underground

By now I understood the Japanese meeting style of each group stating positions with multiple meetings needed to iron out differences before any plan of action could be taken. The process was long and cumbersome. All of us, the USI, USJ Co. teams and the GCs, were acutely aware of maintaining the schedule. However, meetings often bogged down with the GCs wanting to get the work done quickly but with little regard for aesthetics, while USI, charged with guest experience, often resisted all changes which might affect the look of the park.

A major concern in a Japanese-style meeting was "saving face," and to the Japanese, this meant both theirs and ours. The GCs would never directly say "No," just suck their teeth, shake their heads and mutter "is difficult" leaving the USI team to guess the true intent.

Often, our group had alternate methods or acceptable compromises, but because of the "face-saving," these could not be presented directly. Solutions had to be formally proposed by the GCs and accepted by USJ Co. Some method to shortcut this process was required. It was time to go underground.

I had developed a good working relationship with several of the GC people and, following contentious meetings, we began to talk informally. Meeting inconspicuously on the site, we could empathize about the situation. Somewhere in the conversation I might inject something like, "We could save some piping if the twelve-inch water line planned through here could be routed out of sight over there." From these informal conversations, I was also able to learn which tasks were really impossible and not just inconvenient for the GCs.

By the next meeting, USI had a good idea where we might have to back-off on impossible dreams, and often ideas mentioned during these informal walks appeared in the GC's subsequent proposal. Presented as their plans, we could agree, and everyone "saved face." This informal activity greatly reduced the number of follow-up meetings.

Toward the end of the project, our little underground became important for staying on schedule. And we became somewhat bolder, even passing sketches on alternate ideas. It felt a little like back in grammar school passing notes under the table. But it worked.

*   *   *   *   *

In Japan, the group was most important. Individualism was discouraged. There's a Japanese saying which translates to: "The nail which sticks up gets hammered down." Therefore, no Japanese will take a position without group consensus. Following the successful completion of a goal or milestone, it was always the team, not any particular member, to be praised. Congratulations went like this:

————Original Message————
From: Collins, Larry
Sent: Tuesday, October 10, 2000 2:14 PM
To: [Takenaka Team Managers]
Cc: [*JAWS* Attraction Manager}; Bowtie Dave
Subject: *JAWS* Water Transfer

Nishioka-san and Nakaki-san,

Congratulations on the successful water transfer fill of the *JAWS* lagoon on Saturday. Please convey USI's heartfelt thanks to the GC and Kabota teams who made meeting this milestone possible.

I visually inspected the *JAWS* lagoon and water treatment system this morning and noted that the water treatment is on and in full start-up operation. Water flow over the *JAWS* lagoon return weirs[13] is running as expected. Weir height is consistent with no significant high or low spots. We will continue to monitor as it is a good indication of any differential settlement[14] [of the lagoon].

Thank you again for all your help. Job well done!

Larry Collins
Project Engineer
Jurassic Park, *JAWS* & *WaterWorld*
USR Japan Supervision Inc., *Osaka*

These messages went a long way toward maintaining the good working relationship we had developed early in the project.

---

[13] Edge channels around the lagoons like those found around the perimeter of public swimming pools for routing overflow

[14] Because we were building on fill, there was concern that the sinking of the grade—settlement—might be uneven.

Fireworks

Hanabi Taikai (Haan-a-bee Tie-kie)
Fireworks Festival (Literally "grand accumulation of fire flow-ers")
August is fireworks month in Japan. The Japanese believe beauty is fleeting; and fireworks, like the cherry blossom, are exquisite expressions of that concept.

*　　*　　*　　*　　*

Lorna

During the summer, most cities and towns in Japan celebrate a *Hanabi Taikai* or Fireworks Festival. From our balcony we could gaze out over the whole *Kansai* area and see colored lights springing up in the distance from one location or another.

The city of *Takarazuka* staged its largest display downtown on August first and second. The same show was presented on both nights for about an hour. The fireworks were exploded along the *Mukogawa (Muko* River*)* which snaked through the city at the bottom of the hill below our apartment.

Later in the month, there was another display at the *Takarazuka Racetrack* several miles east of our location.

Since we had not moved until a week after the big show in 1998, we missed it. However, in 1999 we invited the whole project team for a fireworks-watching party at our place on Sunday night, August first.

Traditionally, the Japanese wore *yukata* (summer *kimono*) and *zori* (sandals with a toe strap) or *geta* (raised wooden sandals) for watching fireworks. Women wore their hair up so their necks were visible. (This was considered sexy.) And they all carried fans—both men and women—a necessity in the scorching summer heat!

One of the Japanese project assistants decided everyone coming to our party should follow tradition. He even took several team members shopping so they could get the proper outfits.

We were fortunate since I had previously been given presents of beautiful *yukata* by two of our Japanese students. I just had to decide which one to wear.

I had *obi* (colored sash worn with *kimono* or *yukata*) to go with them, too, but wasn't sure how to wrap and tie the thing without help.

Larry had purchased a nice black-and-white *yukata* on an early trip to *Kyoto*. He was teased about it by the Japanese, however, because it was covered in Japanese characters saying *Omedito Gozaimasu* (Congratulations). Apparently it was meant to be worn on a birthday or other special occasion. He didn't care. It was actually large enough to fit him.

A couple of the translators on the project arrived early the day of the party to help the rest of the gals—especially the Americans—tie their *obi*. It was quite an art, and very difficult to learn. We were all grateful for the assistance.

We observed Japanese tradition in our home while in Japan. All footwear, including *zori*, was removed when entering and left in the *genkan*, or vestibule. Close to the front door was a special cabinet to hold shoes. We provided slippers for our guests who wished to wear them.

*   *   *   *   *

We decided on a potluck dinner to keep things easy, and invited everyone to bring something to share. It also helped keep the cost down. No small item when food in Japan was at least twice the cost of the same thing in the US—if it could be found at all. I made a big pot of chili and a green salad.

There was lots of *sushi* and *yakitori* (chicken skewers) and *onagiri* (a seaweed-wrapped triangle of sticky white rice with a "surprise" in the center—poppy seeds, *wasabi*, sour plum, or a morsel of eel or raw fish). Some of the American team brought chips and snack foods, rice crackers and the like. I had ordered a case of salsa from the Foreign Buyers' Club when we first arrived, so we had plenty for parties.

There were desserts, such as the little pancakes often eaten as a sweet. These came as separate rounds the diameter of an orange, or "glued" together with red bean paste. Someone even brought *fugetsudo*, delicate thin cookies from *Kobe*. And there were donuts from the *Mr. Donut* shop near the train station.

We had learned something about Japanese donuts early in our adventure. We had expected these confections from an American company to be the same as those we were used to. However, there were two kinds of donuts in Japan—sweet and "savory." The sweet ones were familiar, if not quite as sugary as those back home. But the "savory" ones were a new experience. The first time Larry bit into what he thought was a jelly-filled treat and tasted curry instead was quite a surprise. Some of the "savory" varieties contained teriyaki beef, sausage or fish fillings.

*   *   *   *   *

There were a number of the Hollywood branch of the team in town on business trips, and they were invited along with those who were relocated. In addition, USJ Co. and the GCs were emailed invitations. And we asked all our Japanese "kids."

We ended up with quite a mix of people. There were several of the GC people (including one with his children), three of our Japanese students with a boyfriend and a couple of their friends in tow, most of the relocated Universal team with their spouses, several from Hollywood, quite a few of the translators and even one couple who were in *Osaka* to select their housing prior to making the move. There were over fifty in all.

As we walked through the place during the evening, we realized the "party house" had become everything we had hoped it would be the first time we saw it. We had envisioned a place where both parts of our lives—American and Japanese—could come together and really get to know each other.

That night we observed our Japanese "daughters" speaking animatedly with our project translators. Both groups were about the same age and had much in common. Some of the conversation was in English, and some in Japanese. They exchanged email addresses and several remain in touch.

The GCs were getting to know more of the people with whom they would be working for the next year and a half.

The Hollywood visitors and potential expatriates were becoming acquainted with the group already there. The newer members of the team were forming relationships with the veterans.

The guy who had been in town to select his housing at the time of the party stopped by my office about a year and a half later. He and his family were returning to California. He shook my hand and said, "I want to thank you for inviting us to your place when we were on our orientation trip. It convinced my wife and me to make the move to *Osaka*. Before seeing how well you had adjusted, we weren't sure we could adapt to the culture and the challenges. I'm glad we came. It's been a great experience for us and our kids."

*   *   *   *   *

Before we arrived, we were told the Japanese didn't invite people to their houses, so, for many of our Japanese guests, a party held in a private residence was a new experience. Get-togethers were usually in restaurants or bars because typical homes were too small for entertaining. The GC and USJ Co. attendees came to many of our future parties and invited others.

Of course, the real attraction for this event was the view of the show from our balcony.

While still in California, we had purchased two round tables and ten chairs to use outside. Our balcony was about ten feet deep and ran most of the length of the front of the apartment. We could easily seat twenty to thirty people there, and on fireworks evenings, we did.

Since we were some distance from the normal watching area along the river where the musical accompaniment could be heard, we put Handel's "Music for Fireworks" on the stereo while the colors burst in the sky.

The Japanese word for fireworks, *Hanabi*, literally means "fire flowers." That night it was easy to see how the name came about. The show was spectacular. What a great experience to be sitting on our balcony with good friends, a breathtaking view of the city lights below and seeing the summer night sky shimmer with explosions of color.

While we were "oohing" and "ahing" at the display, one of the art directors leaned over to me and said, "I love fireworks. But I've never looked down on them before!" He was mesmerized throughout the show. Even after the pyrotechnics ceased, people stayed and visited. No one wanted to leave.

At the end of the evening, our photographer-in-residence, "Bowtie" Dave, decided we should take a group shot. Copies of that print as well as the one taken the following year when we repeated the tradition, hang on my office wall at work. I love being surrounded by these special reminders of the warm friendships and good times we shared during our sojourn in Japan.

✶   ✶   ✶   ✶   ✶

For our guests, getting back down to the *Takarazuka* train station proved daunting. We started our party a couple of hours before the show began. A few people drove, but most of our friends came by train and bus. We should have realized everyone who lived anywhere on the hill with a view of the display would have people over to enjoy it with them.

By the time most were ready to go, the road down the mountain was clogged with people and vehicles. No busses were coming back up the hill to transport folks because they couldn't get through the crush. Larry volunteered to drive as many as he could squash into his van.

A hearty group decided to walk to the station. This took about half an hour at a leisurely pace. On those few days when it was neither too hot nor too cold, we took the stroll ourselves.

One of the gals, however, had decided to get new shoes for the occasion. And not just shoes or *zori*, but *geta*. Those wooden clogs were inflexible, and the toe strap rubbed in the same place with each step. By the time she reached the train, she had huge blisters on her feet, and her arches ached.

The next day at work, she proudly displayed her "war wounds" to everyone. But she also let them know, despite the long hike at the end, she had enjoyed the evening very much.

*   *   *   *   *

We later heard a tale illustrating just how far the Japanese would go to assist those who were lost. One of the people who drove that night managed to make his way through town, but took a wrong turn when leaving. He didn't get too far before he realized the written directions no longer worked. He had three others with him, and all of them poured over the instructions, trying to recall each turn.

As they were doing this, a young man came up to the driver's side window and asked if he could help. The driver, who was Japanese-born and spoke the language, was able to tell their potential savior where they were headed.

"Ah," he said, nodding, recognizing their mistake. Then he offered to show them the way back to their route. He suggested he ride with them until they were safely on track again.

His offer was quickly accepted, and he walked around the car to sit in the front passenger seat, while the person who had been sitting there moved to the back. In the darkness, he had not realized the other three people in the car were big *gaijin* (foreigners).

They later described the various expressions which passed over his face, but, true to his word, he gamely got into the car and went with them. They were sure he feared kidnapping—or worse.

He managed to point out the twists and turns needed to get them safely on course. In the end, there was much bowing and thanks as he headed home, and they continued on their way.

*   *   *   *   *

145

Despite the traffic and crowds, most of the group were enthusiastic about making the trip again the following year. Our fireworks parties remain among our most cherished memories of Japan.

Of Summer and Surf

Longboard
Term used to describe a surfboard ranging from nine to eleven feet in length, compared to a "short board" measuring from five and one-half to eight feet long. The surfboard I rode in Japan measured nine-feet, ten-inches.

*　　*　　*　　*　　*

Larry

In California, I surfed almost every weekend all year 'round and with friends much of the time. In Japan I was only able to surf once a month at most and only during the summer months when the weather was warm. There, surfing for me was a solitary endeavor. I didn't say I was alone. In Japan, it seemed any activity or sport required a crowd. Since I didn't speak the language very well, most conversations with the locals were limited to, "*Ohayo Gozaimasu*" ("Good morning") or "*Surfu sukoshi desu*" ("Surf is small") and an occasional "thumbs up" following a good ride.

My summer surf agenda went like this:

The alarm sounded at 3:00 a.m. It took about half an hour to dress and load the van with a towel, short wetsuit, extra trunks and a couple of chilled plastic bottles of cold drinks. In Japan there were always many choices of non-alcoholic liquid refreshment—several different kinds of green tea ('o-cha'—with and without sugar, with and without milk), smoky Chinese oolong tea (also sweetened or unsweetened), "Pocari Sweat" (a local sports drink favorite that tasted somewhat like ginger ale with milk), "Calpis" (a yogurt-flavored soft drink), and various "vitamin drinks" (loaded with caffeine and nicotine). I also included a two-liter bottle of water and bucket to shower the salt and sand off after surfing.

Then I drove the van down from our assigned spot on top of the seven-floor parking structure to the loading zone in front of the apartment building. Finally, I had to schlep the surfboard down the stairs—all fifteen floors—since it did not fit in the elevator. Then I hit the road.

The first hour of travel was on high-speed toll way from *Takarazuka* through *Osaka*, following the signs to the *Kansai* International Airport at speeds of about one hundred kilometers-per-hour (sixty-two miles-per-hour). My Toyota LiteAce van had a warning bell (sounding like a front door chime) that rang incessantly at any speed above one hundred five kilometers-per-hour. Some people disconnected these alarms, but I left mine intact as I wanted to remain on friendly terms with the highway police. I became amazingly adept at holding the van speed to one hundred four kilometers-per-hour.

Beyond the airport, the road changed from a four-lane toll way to a narrow two-lane highway. Since the mountains in this area ran almost down to the sea, the highway alternately meandered over mountain passes, through tunnels, past rice paddies, through several rustic fishing villages and along the coast. The major landmarks on the way seemed to be several large pachinko parlors of chrome, glass and flashing neon lights. They certainly stood out from the simple wooden shops and houses of the local people. The route roughly paralleled the JR *Hanwa* train line, crossing and re-crossing the tracks. While the drive was pretty, it was not very fast; the remaining twenty-five kilometers took more than an hour to traverse.

Beyond the small village of *Misaki*, the road got even narrower. The first time Lorna and I searched for *Isonora Beach*, the way became so constricted we thought for sure we were on the wrong road. (Approaching cars could not pass each other in many places.) Fortunately, we persevered, finally spotting an *Isonora Beach* sign. We turned left up an even narrower path, no wider than a driveway, past the *Isonora* railway station and found the beach.

One morning my van and another arrived at the station crossing from opposite directions at precisely the same time. As there was no way to turn or backup, we each pulled in our mirrors and eased past the other very carefully, all the while being very polite and apologetic for being in each other's way (much bowing and nodding). Sure a different attitude than I would have expected in a similar situation in the US.

The space between the vehicles while passing was about a quarter inch door-to-door. The distance from my left front tire to the three-foot deep ditch on the side of the road was about half an inch. Most Japanese families going to this beach arrived by train and didn't encounter this problem.

Past the station was a breakwater built between the town and the beach. Parking behind the wall cost ¥800 for all day. It was collected by a very old (she looked about eighty) and bent-over Japanese lady who managed to arrive at my car the instant I stopped. For a good parking space, I had to arrive before 6:00 a.m.

Board in hand, I climbed the stairs over the wall to find a quarter mile long sandy beach between two rock jetties. The distance from the wall to the water was about fifty-yards. The beach above the high tide line was almost entirely covered by tents and corrugated metal stands. These were shops selling everything anyone would need for a day at the beach. There were foods, like the ever-present *yakitori* (chicken-on-a-stick) and *soba* (buckwheat noodle soup), drinks (both hard and soft), sunscreen, clothes, umbrellas, artwork, toys—you name it. This area had a real carnival atmosphere with many colorful flags and signs (advertising, I think) waving from poles planted in, around and on the tents and structures.

Beyond the tents sat the lifeguard stand, manned by an impressive team of immaculately uniformed lifeguards in matching trunks, tank tops and beanie hats, patterned after those of Australian lifesaving clubs. In front of the stand was a large portable reel of rope. A rescuer would take the end of the rope and swim out to a victim. Then the other lifeguards would reel them both safely back to the beach. There were about eight or ten guards at the station. They stood in a straight line in front of the stand, bodies at attention, hands clasped behind backs, eyes scanning out to sea for any sign of trouble. They were all young, energetic and about evenly mixed, men to women.

Surfing was allowed on the entire beach until 8:00 a.m. At that time, half the beach was roped off for swimmers only. Hence, the need to get to the beach by 6:00 a.m. as there were generally about 500 boarders already in the water at sunup. By 8:00 a.m. at least as many swimmers had arrived, so it made sense to separate them.

The swells were generally small (less than three feet when measured from crest to bottom). Rides were short, but plentiful. On my longboard, I could catch waves earlier and farther from shore than the other surfers. The Japanese there were especially polite to me (probably because I was a foreigner) and very interested in my board. Most of them had short boards.

Usually I was through surfing by 8:30 or 9:00 a.m. and would return home to *Takarazuka* around noon, depending on traffic.

The summer surf along the *Wakayama* coast, especially at *Isonora*, was crowded by California standards, but still fun. I did, however, make the mistake the first year of going to the beach on "Marine Day"—July 20, 1999. I learned this was the traditional day when nearly every Japanese family in the entire country went to the beach. Crowds were two to three times normal size. I didn't make the same mistake the following year.

Typhoon Surf

My first big surf opportunity came on *Respect for the Aged Day*—September 15, 1999. The surf report on the Internet indicated a typhoon forming to the southeast which would send some swells into the *Wakayama* area.

When I arrived at *Isonora*, the surf was definitely "overhead" with the peaks of the waves curling over nearly ten feet above the flat area at the bottom. It was big, but too rough and windblown to be ridden by the 500 or so surfers in the water at 6:00 a.m. A five-minute study of the situation told me I did not really want to go out there. Besides, amazingly, the parking attendant had not yet been by to collect the ¥800 parking fee.

I remembered (from a former trip, where I took a wrong turn and got lost) a side road to *Sata Port* where a long left-hand point jutted into the ocean. I thought it might offer some protection from the wind. Normally the surf there was about ankle high but well-shaped for riding. I decided to check it out. On my arrival, I found head-high, windblown and bumpy left-breaking waves wrapping around the point with about twenty surfers in the water braving the elements. I parked along the road next to the cliff overlooking the break where a very bent-over little old lady (looking much like the one from *Isonora*) exacted ¥500. Parking was cheaper in *Sata*.

The beach consisted of the natural rocky point, joined to a manmade breakwater forming the outer wall of a small marina, protecting one hundred or so fishing boats moored inside. Where the point met the breakwater, a small sand beach, about twenty yards long and fifteen feet from cliff to waterline, had formed. The breakwater was constructed from pre-cast concrete pyramid-shaped blocks each about fifteen feet across.

The waves crashed into the breakwater with a tremendous "whump" sound. Any surfboard venturing into that territory was a goner.

I descended narrow eroded concrete stairs to the beach and headed out to the break. The wind was so powerful I had to continuously paddle just to stay in the same place, and if I wanted to move against the wind, needed to stroke even harder. The wind-driven spray from the nose of the board actually stung. Several rides told me I had come to the right place. The left-breaking waves were long and fast with room for several cutbacks. The ones going right were very short and not worth the effort. After an hour, the wind increased to the point where it became extremely difficult to get onto the waves. I caught the last one which could be ridden, and managed to target the small sandy beach. With the wind pushing from behind, it was kind of like landing a jet plane on an aircraft carrier. Others were not so lucky and had a difficult paddle against the wind, past the board-hungry breakwater, to gain the beach. I made it back home around noon, tired but happy.

Respect for the Aged Day—Part 2

September 15, 2000, was the third such holiday I had celebrated since arriving in Japan. Each of the previous years I had surfed on this holiday. This year was no exception. Lorna was in California with our family, so my plan was to spend an entire day in the water.

Since I had no one to hurry home to, I slept until 5:15 a.m., loaded the car, and was away by 6:00 a.m. I thought I would take the expressway north, past *Kyoto* and *Lake Biwako* (or *Biwa*—pronounced 'Bee-Wah'), then head east on Highway 1. This would take me to the north end of the *Nara Prefecture* or even the southern tip of the *Shizuoka Prefecture*. I knew both had good surf. My weather report and Japanese Internet site both indicated the surf would be up.

However, in Japan, my best plans often went awry. No sooner had I left *Takarazuka* headed for *Kyoto*, than the expressway came to a complete halt because of some accident or closure ahead. Unlike in the US, in Japan when an accident occurred and traffic was stopped, the authorities did not let the cars continue until the problem had been removed. So, for the next three hours, all traffic sat in the sun without moving. The air temperature hovered at about 30°C (88°F) and the humidity remained above 90%.

During the long wait, some families abandoned the father to sit in the car while the mother, parasol held high to block the sun, herded the children down the road to find shade, and perhaps sustenance. Men walked to the side of the road to relieve themselves. Car doors were left open and people sat, slept, talked, called on their cell phones and read in the shade of the larger vehicles. I was lucky enough to have picked up the English language *Asahi News* on my way out of the house that morning, so I could pass the time. I read the entire newspaper, including want ads.

I finally made it to the *Kyoto* exit by 9:30 a.m. and decided not to continue as the road ahead was still closed. I paid the first toll (¥1350, about $13) and headed back to *Osaka* where I took the familiar *Hanwa Expressway* toward *Wakayama*. This time I did not turn off for *Isonora Beach* or at *Wakayama* itself, but decided to follow the expressway to the end. I stopped at a rest area for fuel and a snack since I had consumed most of my drinks during the long traffic delay.

Beyond *Wakayama*, the expressway traveled mostly underground. The hills were so steep that tunnels were the only answer. They were quite comfortable since I was protected from the sun and heat. They were pretty straight, well lighted and ventilated. About noon, I exited from the last tunnel at the final tollbooth (at a cost of ¥4200 more). Six hours on the road, and I still hadn't seen the ocean.

The exit was a few kilometers from a coastal town called *Gobo*, another fishing village. There I rejoined Highway 42 as it wound its way along the coast. Turning onto the highway, I saw the ocean for the first time. The waves looked about shoulder high (good for Japan). Now to find a somewhere to surf.

From the highway, I spotted a small half-moon bay with about twenty surfers in the water. Nirvana! Chest high waves broke on either side of the bay, rights on one side, lefts on the other. I parked along the highway near some other obvious surf vehicles. No little old lady to take parking fees? I must really have been out in the country. I put on my wetsuit and headed into the water.

The waves peaked up just outside the bay, then broke in long smooth walls. There was plenty of room for walking the board. (Moving toward the front of the board causes it to trim and ride faster; retreating to the back is necessary to slow, stall and turn.) The best surfers walk, less proficient riders shuffle, here most of the locals just stood in one place for the entire ride.

One other longboarder (better than the rest) and I shared the larger waves and cheered each other on (all without words). I did get one long ride with my foot over the nose of the board (called "hanging five") which brought cheers and much respect from the locals. Once again, I was treated with great courtesy. They would even point to a good wave and indicate I should ride it. There were still plenty for everyone. Two hours of good surfing certainly relieved the frustrations of the morning. I just rode the right-hand waves and never even got over to try the lefts.

About 3:00 p.m., I packed up and left as storm clouds were approaching. I found my way back to the expressway and returned home to *Takarazuka* about 6:30 p.m. It didn't actually begin to rain until I had almost reached *Osaka*.

I spent ten hours on the road for two hours in the water. I heard it wasn't uncommon for Japan.

After Summer

My final trip of the season to *Isonora* was on "Sports Day"—October 11th. The Internet report showed very small surf (less than one meter) for the East Coast. But I talked to a local Japanese surfer at work who insisted the surf would be up. Who was I to question a positive rumor over the opinion of experts?

So, up I bounded at 3:30 a.m., loaded the car, drove two hours, etc., etc. What did I find? The sun was shining. The air temperature was about 90°F. The conditions were glassy and the water temperature registered in the high 70s. Altogether, much nicer than most trips I had made during the summer. The only drawback was the surf was only about one foot high (just as the experts had predicted).

The beach itself had undergone a massive change. When I was there in August, by 6:00 a.m. there were 500 temporary stands set up on the beach. Now, the sand was deserted. Gone were the sellers hawking their wares. Gone were the lifeguards in their uniforms. Gone, the matching swim caps, tank-top shirts and trunks patterned after the outfits worn by Australian lifesaving clubs. Gone were the flags and signs dividing the surfers from swimmers. In fact, there was not a swimmer or non-surfer to be seen. The only life on the beach was about one hundred surfers enjoying the tiny waves, and my now-familiar friend, the little old lady, collecting parking fees (still ¥800).

Small waves made for many short, fun rides. Not much challenge though. The paddle back out took about ten strokes. Some of the short boarders were actually standing in the shallow shore break and just jumping onto a wave as it came by. I could still pick up waves farther out and make a couple of turns before the fin dragged on the sand. I finished surfing about 9:00 a.m. and went to check out the local surf shop, "*Original Surf Boads by Brutus.*" (Yes, that's exactly how the sign was spelled.) A fellow surfer from work had asked me to locate a particular Japanese surfing magazine, so I stopped at the shop to see if they had it. Unfortunately, it didn't open until 11:00 a.m., and I didn't want to hang around that long.

I would eventually meet Brutus. He was a short, stocky Japanese guy with a dark beard who looked a little like the character from the Popeye cartoons. Although he spoke almost no English, he indicated he was given his nickname because of the resemblance. He even used the cartoon character as his logo. Inside his shop was a huge map of the local area showing all the good surf breaks. I wished I had met him sooner and had seen his map before wandering around and only happening upon some of them by accident.

Back home shortly after noon that day, I wasn't too tired. The most exhausting part was the long two and a half-hour return drive, topped off by carrying the surfboard back up the fifteen floors to the apartment.

*   *   *   *   *

After October, the winter set in and the air temperature quickly dropped. It was hard for a native Californian like me to accept that a place so hot in the summer could turn so cold during the winter. Within several weeks, the daytime high temperature had dropped from 90°F to below freezing.

It was time to hang up the board and wetsuit for another season.

The Tree Saga—

Or Have You Ever Seen a Grown Man Cry?

Sumimasen (sue-mee-mah-sen)
Polite word meaning "I am sorry" or "Excuse Me" and also
"Thank You" if the person was inconvenienced. It was a handy
all purpose word to be used when entering a room or meeting or
elevator, and also when concluding a transaction in a shop or
store.

*　　　　*　　　　*　　　　*　　　　*

The landscaping of a theme park was critical to creating the illusions intended to convey the storyline of the attractions. In *Jurassic Park*, for instance, the guest's impression of being in the Costa Rican rainforest (just like in the movie) was indicated in great part by all the plant life in view. The area around the *JAWS* attraction was intended to look like the East Coast of the United States, and the planting around the ride was chosen to further the feeling. This same attention to detail permeated the entire project.

*　　　　*　　　　*　　　　*　　　　*

Several years prior to the scheduled park opening, teams of landscape architects began working with the facility architects and the general contractors (GCs) on the overall layout. The major attractions were positioned along with the restaurants and retail shops. All the infrastructure, utilities, sound systems and lighting were estimated and sketched in. The streets, walkways and accesses were added. Then the locations for all the plants were determined.

Each tree and shrub was located, specified and numbered. Every numbered item was shown on a drawing, as well as a master list, including the type, color and size.

Although some plant material was obtained locally in the *Osaka* area, several trips were made to nurseries in southern *Kyushu* in order to select the tropical plants for *Jurassic Park* and other places where warm climate foliage was specified. (In the dead of the *Osaka* winter of 1998, there were lots of volunteers for those trips!) The team attempted to select plants acclimated to an area close to the site. Then a complicated schedule was established to provide the best conditions for transplanting and nurturing the incoming greenery.

Mature trees were selected as the focal points for several attractions. These large specimens were among the first items to be installed in the park. This was necessary because enormous cranes were required to lift them off the flatbed trucks on which they arrived and position them. Once the parking lots, waterways, streets, buildings and other elements were installed, it would be impossible to gain access again for replacement.

Because these full-grown trees would take time to adjust to the *Osaka* climate, they needed additional attention once they were positioned. And a small percentage were likely to fail anyway simply because of the shock of transplantation.

Our buying teams were excited when they found some large specimen trees with vines and succulents attached. They were overgrown, and that's just how we wanted them! The beards on the large palms hadn't been trimmed, and they had precisely the natural "jungle" look hoped for. Since most of the "extras" would normally have been trimmed for shipping, our team spent a great deal of time and effort in making sure the trees would arrive just as they were found in the nurseries.

The landscaper for *Jurassic Park* (known as "Jurassic Mark") had learned his lesson in this regard the hard way while working on Universal Islands of Adventure in Florida. He was also responsible for the landscaping of the *Jurassic Park* ride there.

In order to make a dramatic statement at the entrance to the attraction, he had hunted throughout Florida for a spectacularly large banyan tree. After visiting quite a few nurseries, he finally located an exceptional specimen. There were three huge branches flowing up out of the trunk, each spreading gracefully in a different direction. The branches were lush and curved, and the roots were prominent. This was just the symbol required to set the stage for guests entering the queue lines.

The tree was purchased. Arrangements were made for shipment. On the appointed day, Mark was on hand as the truck arrived. But when the cover was removed, he discovered to his horror that two of the three large branches had been sawn off. When he asked why, he was told, "It was too large to ship that way."

The banyan was rejected, and the hunt for a replacement began again, knowing whatever they found could never equal the first.

Fortunately, the Japanese translators somehow managed to convey the idea well; the nurseries packed and shipped the plants as specified; the shippers also followed directions; and finally the initial deliveries began. There was great excitement when the first group of tall specimens was set in place. There they stood—the only vertical fixtures with color in the moonscape of brown dirt and enormous craters in the ground.

*   *   *   *   *

In *Jurassic Park* the big trees were of particular concern because they were tropical and needed to adjust to *Osaka's* scorching, humid summers and brutally cold winters. Since most of them were species of palm, they preferred a tropical climate.

Jurassic Mark spent many hours tending, watering and fretting over the largest ones. And most of them did quite well.

As further shipments of smaller foliage arrived, Mark couldn't spend quite as much time on individual plants. He was handling the landscaping for *JAWS* as well, and both of these attractions were vegetation-intensive.

As time went on, he began to notice some of the larger trees withering. Since the permanent irrigation systems were still being installed, he faithfully hauled buckets and long hoses about the huge beds to be sure everything was adequately watered. He would arrive on the site early in the morning to inspect his area and assure himself that all the plants received the moisture they required.

At last, the irrigation system was installed, tested and operational. At that point, Jurassic Mark thought most of his problems were over. The large trees seemed to be doing well, and it was time to start concentrating on the rest of the shrubs and groundcover.

Suddenly, however, the trees started dying. The big ones. It took a while to figure out why, and before he did, one or two were lost. It seems no budget or time was allocated for irrigation in the overall project plan until after park opening—over a year away! When he asked about the lack of irrigation, he received the answer, "Ah, yes, Mark-san, but it hasn't rained," as if that explained everything.

Of course, there were urgent meetings and much persuading, pleading, begging and groveling trying to get the GCs to agree that watering the foliage was necessary.

Unfortunately their answer to the loss of the trees was to replace them with bamboo. Now, bamboo is attractive and tropical, but it doesn't have the same visual impact as the large specimens. Those in question were also very expensive and their loss had a huge impact on the budget.

By the time all the negotiations, endless meetings, apologies, bows and "*sumimasens*" were concluded, a couple more of the large trees were lost, and it was no longer possible to replace them in kind. In order to retain the untouched rainforest feel however, Jurassic Mark was quite specific. All dead foliage was to be left in place as it would be in the real locale. The Japanese were rather taken aback by this request, but the maintenance team felt so badly about the losses, they left the dead plant life alone. (Whether or not they had plans to sneak in later and remove it will never be known.)

The struggle over irrigation and bamboo continued for several months during which time the landscaping suffered even more. However, since Jurassic Mark was still taking personal interest in the specimen trees, those that did survive flourished—with all their vines and additional flora intact.

*   *   *   *   *

There is a tradition observed on every construction project called the "Topping-Off Ceremony." This is when the highest steel beam is set in place. In the case of USJ, the highest beam was at the top of the *Jurassic Park* show building. (This is the spot above the eighty-five-foot boat drop at the end of the ride.)

For this occasion, in October of 1999, the press and local dignitaries were invited. The local Shinto priest was scheduled to perform a blessing; the TV cameras would roll; and a helicopter would fly in the final beam and set it into place. Additional helicopters were in the air covering the event for TV, and a couple more handled security. This was such an exclusive occasion that we, the team actually working on the project, were specifically forbidden to attend. We had to watch the whole thing on television later in the evening.

For several days ahead of the ceremony, the area was thoroughly cleaned. All signs of trash, dirt and debris were removed. Several large tents were erected to house all the VIPs.

Early the morning of the ceremony, the Area 3 group made one last visit to *JP* to be sure everything was in readiness.

When they reached the ride area, they couldn't believe their eyes. In typical Japanese fashion, all the trees had been manicured. The "beards" had been removed from the palm trees. All the extra vines and additional foliage had been stripped away, and the dead plant life had disappeared. The trunks on all the trees were slick and smooth, and the fronds on the palms had been neatly and symmetrically shaped. The entire jungle look which had been so carefully cultivated was now gone. It would take several years before the lush rainforest illusion could possibly return. And we didn't have that much time before park opening. (The area henceforth was known among team members as "Jurassic Bonsai," much to Jurassic Mark's consternation.)

Never before—or afterward—did we see Mark so close to tears. It was as if he were in shock. He simply couldn't believe what he beheld. All his careful nurturing was now gone. The rest of us said soothing words and quietly and gently removed him from the area. But he continued to mourn his lost jungle until his departure from Japan. And even the sincere "*sumimasens*" from the Japanese maintenance team could never make up for the loss.

*   *   *   *   *

Addendum:

In a recent communication with Jurassic Mark about this painful incident, he told us the following:

"I received an email from one of my Sumitomo Forestry friends who said he was in Jurassic Park—the Ride a few months ago and was sorry to say that a couple of the largest Phoenix palms were now dead."

So the story continues...

Terrazzo Wars

Keiretsu (kāy-rett-sue)
A family of businesses working together with exclusive relation-ships to enhance every member

*   *   *   *   *

Lorna

Theme parks have streets, walkways, lobbies, floors and sidewalks known as "hardscape." Due to the volume of traffic every day, only the sturdiest materials can be used in these areas.

Once we moved to the jobsite, a sample program for this material began. Vendors arrived to create one-meter-by-one-meter examples of their work. Once approved by USJ Co. and the art direction team, these would be moved to the area where the actual installation would occur to be used as models.

For *Jurassic Park* and the western area, "designer dirt" was fabricated. It had to look like the real thing, but be sturdy enough to stand up under the wear and tear of over one million visitors each month. The material of choice was colored concrete. In the *JP* area, large cracks were gouged to show age. Then dinosaur tracks were stamped into the wet surface. When completed, the finished product looked like an ancient site, recently uncovered.

In the western area, the dyed concrete was stamped with the impressions of cowboy boots, horseshoes and wagon ruts.

Even the beaches on Amity Island were fake. The concrete base was textured and colored to resemble sand. Bits of shell and pebbles were imbedded in the surface. Then real people (members of the USI and *Takenaka* teams willing to remove their shoes on a cold wintry day) stomped around on the partially cured surface to achieve the look of a populated beach. Of course, each foot placement occurred under the watchful eye of the Area 3 assistant art director, Michael, whose orders included:

"Larry, one more lap around the fire pit…Take longer strides…Now, walk on your tiptoes…Everyone move toward the changing cabanas…Okay, now spread out and go different directions…"

The whole process took about an hour, at the end of which, feet were icy. But the sand looked real.

*　　*　　*　　*　　*

Terrazzo[15] was specified for many locations because of its beauty and durability. With relatively little maintenance, it would remain attractive for a long time. Many early design decisions were made on the basis of using poured terrazzo. It was cheaper than marble but would provide a similar appearance. Its advantage over marble or other stone was it could be replaced or repaired as necessary. Since some of the fixtures on theme park floors may be moved from time to time, this was an important consideration.

One of the areas of terrazzo concentration was on the "Hollywood Boulevard" walk of fame. Universal obtained licensing to reproduce the same star designs used on those famous sidewalks. Even before construction began on the buildings, the metal bases with the embedded stars and symbols for our version of this landmark were being cast by the same foundry which makes the real ones in Hollywood.

The pre-cast metal bases were shipped to Japan. Then the distinctive terrazzo surrounding the star design would be poured and polished after the framework was in place on the sidewalks.

*　　*　　*　　*　　*

Terrazzo was used in Japanese construction. We had seen it in many different locations. Each time we went to the *Osaka* World Trade Center (WTC), we walked on the smooth, seamless poured terrazzo floor. However, in most locations it was installed as prefabricated tiles, finished in a factory.

Concerns were raised in our weekly staff meeting about a lack of terrazzo samples.

"Have the GCs located a vendor to install the terrazzo yet?" asked "Bowtie" Dave, the A&E director, one Monday morning.

"Not yet," answered Berj, the director of area development. "Our specifications have been given to the GCs, and we've asked them to come up with a list

---

[15] A man-made stone composed of chips of marble, mixed with cement or epoxy and then polished. Terrazzo is poured, troweled out, hardened, ground down and burnished on site to make a surface that is vibrant, long lasting and durable.

161

31 Months in Japan

of potential suppliers so we can make a selection. They say we should have workers arriving next week to begin the test pieces."

"Great," Dave responded, and the meeting moved on to the next issue.

Examples from some vendors finally arrived, but all were factory-made and would not work in our applications. The team began researching companies on the GC's recommended list, attempting to locate craftsmen who could install terrazzo on-site. Again and again the answer came back: they could only provide it as prefabricated tiles.

Since "Hollywood Boulevard" required poured terrazzo, pre-made squares were not an option. And, although this was the most critical and visible location of concern, there were other areas of the park where terrazzo had been specified and where alternatives suggested by the GCs couldn't be used.

Several weeks later, the action item was back on the agenda.

"Any luck with the terrazzo?" asked Dave.

"Not yet," answered Berj. "They say they're working on it, but I have a feeling the real delay is because they don't have a relationship with anyone who does it the way we're requesting. You know about *Keiretsu*. I suspect there are people who can do on-site installations, but our GCs probably don't have formal relationships with them. They keep trying to convince us the factory-cast alternative would work."

"Do you think we can find a way to get them to consider bringing in someone outside their alliance?" asked Dave.

"At this point, that's our advice to them," Berj replied with a shrug of his shoulders.

*　　　*　　　*　　　*　　　*

We knew about *Keiretsu*. The concept had made its way to the US as "strategic alliances," but in Japan it related to a more fundamental cultural approach to just about everything. The group was preeminent in all Japanese dealings. Business relationships were formed as exclusive liaisons. These were considered sacrosanct, and companies only did business with other firms in their *Keiretsu*.

The early expats found out the hard way about this practice when we were offered Direct TV as the only choice for a satellite provider since the company supplying the furniture, appliances and other services for Universal had a *Keiretsu* relationship with them.

Then the Area 2 project engineer arrived. He had lived in Europe where Sky Perfect was popular. Before coming to Japan, he had researched this system and discovered it was obtainable and offered more English language programming.

As soon as he got to *Osaka*, he insisted on Sky Perfect. It was finally provided it, but reluctantly. The Universal relocation team was not very popular with their business contacts, but later arrivals were given a choice of satellite company.

*   *   *   *   *

Week after week, the search went on for someone to install the terrazzo as specified in the original design. More vendors submitted samples—of prefabricated tiles. The workmanship was acceptable, but what we really needed was someone to install the material on-site. The action item remained open.

"I know our agreement was to use Japanese vendors whenever possible," said Dave, "but we don't seem to be getting any viable sources."

"My team has gone to vendor locations farther from *Osaka* for demonstrations. However, all these visits have ended in disappointment. When we arrive, we discover all they're producing is the same old prefab tiles," reported Berj. "A couple of suppliers have agreed to come to the site in the next couple of weeks to produce samples. I'll let you know what happens."

"You don't sound too optimistic," observed Dave.

"I'm hopeful, but so far the results haven't been encouraging," was the reply.

Craftsmen came to the jobsite and attempted to create the results we were looking for, but they were uniformly unsatisfactory. The same workmen who could produce a beautiful finished tile in their factories created uneven and inadequate product on-site.

The clock was ticking and park opening was getting closer. Each week in our staff meetings the reports on the search for terrazzo continued to be disappointing.

"It's starting to look like the vendors are deliberately delaying the qualification process hoping that, in the end, we'll simply agree to take whatever they offer," reported Berj after yet another failed demonstration.

"I've worked on several projects here in Asia before," someone in the group volunteered. "We used on-site terrazzo, and the quality was excellent. I may even have the names of a few contacts in my old records."

"Great," said Dave. "Give them to Berj. Maybe we can mention looking outside Japan."

So the threats began.

With the blessing of Universal management, inquiries were made to see what bringing workers from elsewhere in Asia to complete the job would cost.

Of course we knew who the true masters of terrazzo were—the Italians. So we also threatened to get bids from Italian craftsmen for the installation. As might be expected, this option was very expensive. USJ Co. and the GCs balked.

Time was running out. The GCs continued to stall while promising to produce Japanese workers capable of doing the job. And the patience of the Universal team grew short as opening day grew near.

The "Hollywood Boulevard" stars became a major issue. The sidewalks had to be finished so the rest of the street could be "dressed." And the stars were still empty shells waiting to be installed and completed.

Discussions began with Hollywood about sending the stars back to get them finished as terrazzo-filled squares. But more time and budget would be required. There was even a brief suggestion of omitting them from the park altogether. The art directors wouldn't hear of it.

Finally a few of our more resourceful team members worked behind the scenes with a couple of their counterparts on the GC team. They had formed alliances with individual members of the GC construction groups and were able to convince them we weren't going to settle for prefab tiles or poorly poured terrazzo. Those contacts ultimately located a company not on our original list which could produce the desired results.

After months of being told it was "very difficult" (meaning: "*impossible*") accompanied by much sucking of teeth, our persistent Japanese friends unearthed skilled craftsmen who could do the job—and do it well.

There was cheering and back slapping at the staff meeting the morning Berj reported, "The site tests are complete and acceptable. The samples have passed, and we have a commitment for the start of installation of the stars and other floors and sidewalks next week."

The work was closely inspected to be sure we received the caliber of craftsmanship required to duplicate the look of the real Hollywood Boulevard in California. In the end, we achieved our objective.

After seeing the completed work, "Bowtie" Dave observed, "We actually managed to get the Japanese to work outside their normal alliances to create something perfectly American-looking, even though they really didn't want to. It was a tough fight, but I feel exhilarated and triumphant."

The sidewalks were beautiful—complete with terrazzo and brass stars that looked just like the originals.

Attraction 650 DSR...

The Show That Never Was

Kawaii (Ka-wa-i-i)
A Japanese word meaning "cute" favored by teenage girls and conveyed in a high-pitched tone whenever used—which was often

*   *   *   *   *

The concept was born after a meeting a little more than a year before the project was complete. This is how the Area 3 scheduler, Casey, tells the story:

"This is how it began. We were finishing up a weekly team meeting with Takenaka and we were talking about the restaurants. I had just gotten the schedule from Food Services earlier in the day showing when they were going to do training and testing in the kitchens (a.k.a. free food). So the question was asked, 'When do we get to eat in the restaurants?'

I said, 'I know that,' pulled out my schedule and said, 'October 15th.'

Now here is where the whole sordid affair began. The Area 3 art director, *Newman, asked, 'When do we get to watch movies in the theater?' I looked at him with an incredibly blank look.

He responded, 'You know, in the Amity Theater, Building 650.'

Before we got back to the compound, it had degenerated to a stage. And the rest is history."

Thus began one of the best continuing gags of the project.

*   *   *   *   *

Each of the buildings in the park was given a number designation during the design phase. The actual names were finalized before Universal Studios Japan (USJ) opened, but some of them had working names which would change during the course of construction. Area 3 used the 500 and 600 series. We often used the building numbers in our discussions.

The two originators began exchanging emails regarding this "non-attraction." Soon others heard about it and became involved. The working title became the *Dancing Shark Spectacular*, later evolving into the *Dancing Shark Revue*—or "*DSR*" for short.

Here is a sampling of that email record:

March 23, 2000
(From Casey to selected team members and the painting supervisor, *Alan)
Subject: Potential Slip
  *Art [Area 4 attraction manager] just informed me that *Senyo* is having difficulty with the Shark High Kick mechanism for the *650 Dancing Shark Spectacular* and it's interfering with their production of the Water Ride Vehicles for Snoopy. Not that Snoopy is our problem, but they are having trouble with the mechanism and haven't informed us. This is a problem. I suggest we get our responsible engineer and set up a meeting to review the current status.

March 23, 2000
(From Alan to others in Area 3)
Subject: RE: Potential Slip
  Just to confirm your concerns, Casey, I have repeatedly been asking *Senyo* for finish samples for both 650 sets and Snoopy elements. Last week they sent me a beagle with fins and a white shark with a black nose. They just don't get it.
  Perhaps we need to elevate these issues to a higher authority?
  I await instructions to proceed.

April 6, 2000
(From the facility-assistant art director, *Donny, to Alex in HR with copies to team members)
Subject: HR Crisis for 650 Shark Review
  Alex, please help us locate Bobby Darin impersonators in *Osaka*. (You know, to perform the tune "Mack the Knife.") We are actively seeking an individual who acts, sings and looks like Bobby Darin. Actually, anyone who knows the words or

has a copy of the sheet music would probably do. You might hold auditions to see who can sing the most lyrics without lapsing into nonsense or humming. Please get right on this! Construction schedule has the tank, stage and aquarium auditorium finished soon. Rehearsals cannot be too far off.

Frantically yours,
Donny

April 6, 2000
(From Alex to Donny and others)
Subject: RE: HR Crisis for 650 Shark Review

Donny, I will start the search immediately. I have been informed there is a reclusive group of Bobby Darin impersonators living in an abandoned aquarium on the northern tip of Hokkaido. It may bust our budget, but have heard that they can be enticed to make the move to *Osaka* with free bow ties.

In the meantime I suggest we all start practicing just in case.

Casey—Please make sure *Senyo* puts the safety on the high kick mechanisms near the stage. I have had a hard time arranging auditions for the 650 Shark Review ever since one accidentally fired and sent a steel drum player into the fishing nets.

April 7, 2000
(From Donny to Alex and team)
Subject: RE: HR Crisis for 650 Shark Review

Alex, throw in a tube of *Brylcreme* and pocket comb, and get these boys down out of the cold and onto the stage. If they can't sing, see if they can fit into the *Amity Village People* costumes. We still need the sailor, Indian and construction worker characters filled and musical talent is not a necessity.

*   *   *   *   *

At this point, we created some "sample" resumes for various sharks with entertainment experience (e.g. the shark from *JAWS*—deemed too old and tired, a shark from *Flipper*, etc.). They were submitted to HR from a "talent agent."

*   *   *   *   *

April 7, 2000
(From Hamachan, food services manager to Lorna)
Subject: RE: HR Crisis for 650 Shark Review
By the way—Can we get another food cart in front of the Project 650 entrance?

April 18, 2000
(From Casey to the office manager, *Josh with copies to a growing list)
Subject: Lighting Designer
Josh, in your new position as attraction manager of the *650 Dancing Shark Review*, please make sure we have a suitable location for our new Lighting Designer, *Mick. He won't be here all the time, so some sharing might be acceptable. In addition, we have several issues requiring your immediate attention, i.e., Bobby Darin impersonators, shark wranglers, delays in production of the *Senyo* high kick mechanisms, etc. Please see Alex for background on these and other issues requiring your attention. By the way, thank you so much for volunteering for this critical position as we are at the phase of the project where your expertise in live shark shows in Hawaii will be invaluable. Your acceptance will allow Newman, Alex, the rest of the team, and me much more time to do the jobs we were hired for.

If you have any questions, feel free to ask. Regards, Casey

April 18, 2000
(From Newman to Casey and Josh with copies to even more of the group)
Subject: RE: Lighting Designer
Bear in mind we take inordinate pride in designing to a budget and building to a schedule. We've been into this for 9 months, so please make your budget and schedule align with where we are going to wind up—then nobody loses face (win-win, etc.)

Welcome aboard.

PS, Casey, it is a *Revue* in the Parisian sense.

April 25, 2000

(From the Area 4 assistant art director, known as "Cambria-Cat" to Newman and Casey, CCs to team)

Subject: 650 Show Wardrobe

Greetings, Newman and Casey,

In accordance with the latest schedule mitigation requirements, I am notifying you both officially that we have further schedule slip on the shark wardrobe program.

Specifications clearly stated the shark suits were to be form-fitting yet accommodating of various sizes and forgiving of movement since many acrobatics will be required especially the high-kick sequence. Reference: section 7.13 paragraph 2.

I pursued Newman's suggestion of the shape-shifting auto-fit Kevlar/spandex with *memory stretch* combo and it is on backorder. The supplier also indicated any fastening system such as Velcro or zippers is not compatible with this fabric. The costumes, therefore, must be designed to be pulled over the shark's head and body thereby increasing the time for costume changes during the show and causing negative effects to hairstyles and hairpieces. That's the least of my worries at this point.

Please note: the pull-on style also requires elimination of integral booties as required by section 7.13.

Donny: Can we accommodate bootie decrease with some sort of Birkenstock style slip-on or possibly Ugg Boots? I'm trying to stay with the surfer theme for the water ballet gang.

Any and all ideas are welcome. I'd like to add the Kevlar/spandex combo would be the best material to accommodate most of our needs, even with the schedule slip. It is available in a wide variety of Hawaiian prints which have color shifting and black-light capabilities as required by the 3D cabaret gag.

Thanks for your attention to this matter.

Cambria-Cat

PS, I have located maribou boas locally in the *Shinsaibashi* Area, so no further action is required. I will have color samples for your approval within the month. All team members are invited to attend the selection meeting. We will have small, medium and large samples for everyone to try.

April 26, 2000
(From Josh to Newman, Cambria-Cat and Casey with copies to the group)
Subject: RE: 650 Show Wardrobe

I have just finished an important phone call that could have glorious financial and budget burgeoning ramifications that will resound and resonate while rotating the rot that has taken over our beloved 650 show.

Spielberg is filming "Memoirs of a Geisha" here in Kyoto next year. His agent has contacted me about the possibility of using the 650 show in their project. They have offered to pick up the tab for the total build cost, with the understanding that they get to choose the sharks. This picture is budgeted at $100 million. The current budget shows we are in desperate need of funding. Without it, we will never make soft opening. We need the Spielberg money if we have any hope of finishing this important 19th attraction on time.

I understand some of you may oppose "selling out" the original concept. What do you all think about this drastic change?

Your input is requested.

April 27, 2000
(From Cambria-Cat to Newman, Josh and Casey. Copies etc.)
Subject: RE: 650 Show Wardrobe

Please confirm, then, if I need to postpone next month's maribou work session. The vendors were very excited about participating in the project and were planning on bringing free samples of the latest ice blue eye shadow as well as a mega-heel boot which could fill the gap caused by our bootie decrease.

Thanks for the support everyone!

April 27, 2000
(From Casey to Newman, Cambria-Cat and Josh, and copies...)
Subject: RE: 650 Show Wardrobe
Cambria-Cat, I know it's not my area of expertise, but are the maribou boas they plan on showing waterproof? Will they hold their feathery shape and texture even after getting soaked or will there have to be some changes in script/choreography to accommodate changing or switching out of the boas?

It's nice to know that even though we're not getting much support from USI costuming, or many other disciplines for that matter, we've got everyone pitching in on all areas to make this show a success. Josh, I'd consider team jackets if I were you. This group is really pulling together.

Regards, Casey

April 28, 2000
(From Cambria-Cat to Newman and Josh with copies to the usual cohorts)
Subject: Team Jacket
As requested, I'm attaching the concept sketch for the 650 Show Official Team jacket. It is, of course, the first submittal of any USJ Team Wear. Any and all comments are requested. Should it be anorak style or waist fitted? I'm all for shoulder pads. I also think the idea of a chest emblem or patch which squirts water would be especially handy in those all-too-serious work sessions.

I look forward to your comments!

May 16, 2000
(From Lorna to Cambria-Cat with copies to a continuously expanding list)
Subject: RE: Team Jacket
I agree jackets would definitely be an incentive for the team to get this attraction moving ahead. Do you think something either waterproof or water-resistant would be appropriate? What about color? In keeping with the focus of the

attraction (the sharks) it would seem that a blue-gray would be the color of choice. However, we would need a colorful logo. Are you still favoring the original concept design you created some time ago? (And the squirting water button sounds just the thing.)

As for the Spielberg tie-in, I have some doubts about whether or not they would really underwrite the attraction once they understand the story line and "Vegas-style" theming which has been the concept until now. Somehow I can't see changing to a more traditionally Japanese theme at this point in order to conform to the film. I'm sure Spielberg would want the sharks in *kimono* and wigs. Somehow this doesn't work—especially with all your efforts at researching costumes. And getting *geta* [Japanese wooden shoes] the right size could also pose a problem, to say nothing of the *tabi* [Japanese socks].

However, what about the possibility of adding a traditional Japanese number featuring costuming consistent with the movie?

I just talked to Michael [Area 3 assistant art director] re: team jackets. His son lives in Korea and said the jackets can be made very cheaply. You might want to talk to him about getting them there since he has the connection. (He also suggested waterproof material.)

By the way, who is writing the show? I know we are very short-handed and everyone is doing double and triple duty with all the other attractions. It seems we really need to define the overall concept before we finalize the costumes.

I'm really impressed with the work you have done. Congratulations!

By the way, do you know if anyone ever got back to *Hamachan* on his food cart?

Is there power in the area? What about the signs, lighting, graphics, menu boards? Is there an issue with handicapped access? What about food and drink inside the arena? They are ready to pour concrete and we haven't seen any drawings from the GC yet on any of these items.

If there is anything we can do to assist you in getting this project moving at a faster pace, please let us know.

May 16, 2000
(From *Charlie, interiors principal, to Lorna and Cambria-Cat, with copies, etc.)
Subject: RE: Team Jacket
Josh has neglected to update you on the latest developments. We no longer have an ordinary food cart; we are now a full table service food facility. I am rather vague on how we are going to accomplish a Dinner Theater Show as opposed to a simple review, but that's not my department. My job is to deliver the retail and food facilities. For which I am requesting AGAIN the footprints for BOTH facilities.

May 16, 2000
(From Hamachan to Charlie, Lorna and Cambria-Cat, with copies…)
Subject: RE: Team Jacket
Dinner theater show??? The gods have answered us.

You know us guys—we are looking for the easy way out. We are currently in negotiation to purchase for pennies on the dollar Spielberg's failed attempt at a restaurant called "Dive." (It did take a dive, no pun intended.) We were hoping it would be possible to dump one of their submarine-shaped restaurants into a lagoon and call it a day.

Can this be incorporated into your show?

*Lana [merchandise director], any ideas from Merchandise for 650?

May 17, 2000
(From Charlie to the entire bunch)
Subject: RE: Team Jacket
Now I'm the one out of the Loop!

I didn't know the Sub Snack Bar had been nixed. Ya' miss one meeting and look what happens. Who is the coordinator on this project?

Lana: When are we going to be able to get together on the "Shark Fin Baby Boutique"? Remember it's the 1200 sq. ft. retail space attached to the Adopt-A-Shark facility. *Nicole [Area 3 show producer] is on the phone bugging me about the concept every morning. Before I give it to her, I would like to run it by you. Let me know a time. Kit [Area 3 interiors] and I will come and you can buy lunch.

May 17, 2000
(From Clarita [Area 4 interiors] to Kit, copies to Charlie and Lana)
Subject: RE: Team Jacket
I am looking for the Interiors Floor Fixtures document Charlie issued back in February for facility 650. The positions for some of the 3D characters changed. Lana wants to use some of those originally designed for the gondolas [merchandise displays] in the Shark Fin Baby Boutique.

#3D-104	Wild Dancing Shark
#3D-200	Sports Shark (needs logo **baseball cap**)
#3D-184	The Salsa Lover
#3D-88	Babaloo Tropical Shark
#3D-91	Shark Movie Director (**T-shirt** should match the **baseball cap** of the Sports Shark)

Merchandise wants to use them? Where? Please advise because the GC is saying the location of those characters is not clear and it will impact the construction schedule. Thank you.

May 17, 2000
(From Charlie to Clarita and Kit, copies to Lana, and on, and on...)
Subject: RE: Team Jacket
I thought we got rid of the Salsa Lover & replaced it with the shark in *kimono* & wig. Let's make up our minds here people. Nicole is standing over in the corner tapping her foot, and we all know what that means.

A logo for the jackets was ultimately selected—a shark in a Hawaiian shirt drinking from a glass with an umbrella in it.

In keeping with the shark theme, a baseball-style jacket in shiny gray fabric was selected. The hood surrounded by shark teeth was abandoned.

Michael's wife went to Korea and had the jackets custom made there. Since the official budget was still tight and the attraction remained underground, team members paid for their own jackets. They became one of the most enjoyed and prized souvenirs from the project.

Keep in mind—we still finished this project ahead of schedule, under budget and understaffed. And the laughs we shared in the planning of this non-attraction helped get us through some rough places.

*   *   *   *   *

But the fun didn't end with the completion of the park. On April 28, 2002 we received the following from Hamachan:

> I am sitting in Narita airport writing this email. I look outside the lounge window and there sits the *Pokemon*-painted ANA plane right next to, yes you are correct, the *650 DSR Jabberjaw*-painted United jumbo jet. What a beauty!
>
> I am back in Japan right now on a consulting assignment. From the popularity of *650 DSR,* they are talking about adding more food carts in the additional queue area. The Japanese cannot stop squealing, *"Kawaii"* [Cute!]! They cannot keep the *DSR-650* merchandise on the shelves. The dancing shark costume was last year's Halloween favorite for young and old alike.
>
> Thanks to all the design team for making this an experience I, and the Japanese, will never forget.
>
> Warmest Regards,
> *Hamachan*
> Manager, Food Service Administration
> *650 DSR* Alum

Friendship

Tomodachi (tow-mow-da-chee)
Friend

Lorna

The concepts of "*uchi*" and "*soto*" which dominated the culture were explained in a book I read in preparation for our move. "*Uchi*" meant "inside." You were "*uchi*" with your family; but few others fell into that circle. "*Soto*" meant "outside." By definition, all *gaijin* (foreigners) were "*soto.*"

Misayo Igo apparently never read the book.

*   *   *   *   *

Obon was the most revered of all Japanese festivals. It was believed the spirits of dead ancestors returned to their homes at this time. Throughout the country, people traveled to their towns of origin where they prayed at the local shrine and honored their forebears. It was a sort of nation-wide family reunion.

The highlight of the *Obon* celebration was the *Odori* or folk dance festival. The most famous was the *Awa Odori* held in *Tokushima* on *Shikoku* Island.

During the spring of 2000, *Misayo*-san invited us to travel to *Shikoku* Island to celebrate *Obon* with her relatives. This was a private time, reserved for family. And we were invited. Not only that, we were asked to stay in her mother's home in the little town of *Mikamo* because, by then, we were *tomodachi*, friends.

*   *   *   *   *

We arrived at *Misayo's* mother's house at 1:00 a.m. after a four-hour drive fighting holiday traffic. She had waited up. The best room had been prepared for us. She had even purchased long *futon* (sleeping mats) for us because she'd heard Larry was tall. And there were western-style pillows rather than the traditional rice husk Japanese ones.

Since it was so late, we went straight to bed. There would be time for exploring in the morning.

*   *   *   *   *

At 7:00 a.m. there was a loud jingle playing from the community PA system outside, followed by a five-minute announcement. Larry and I laughed thinking it would probably only be attempted for one day in the US. On the second day, the speakers would be gone. This morning wake-up call happened every day in *Mikamo*. *Kazue* had warned us about it and told us to go back to sleep. We did.

When we finally got up a little after 8:00, *Misayo's* mother, *Kuniko*, was already busy making breakfast: rice, *miso* soup, cold cooked vegetables, fried eggs and salmon. After breakfast and a shower, we explored *Kuniko's* home.

THE HOUSE

The entrance was through a sliding glass door facing what looked like the back yard. In the *genkan* (entry), we removed our outdoor shoes and donned house slippers.

A step up about one and one half feet led to a room with a wooden floor, housing only a piano. On the same wall as the piano was a door leading to the kitchen.

To the left, up a step of about eight inches, was the first room. Since *tatami* (straw core with soft reed cover) covered the floor, we removed the slippers worn in the piano room before walking on the mats. This area was about sixteen feet deep and twelve feet wide and contained no furniture. Beyond was the second *tatami* room of about the same size where we slept.

This room had photos of the *Misayo's* father, grandparents and a great uncle on the wall, protecting us as we slept. There was a traditional alcove or *tokonoma* on the back wall. The *tokonoma* usually featured a display of flowers, artwork or other treasures. We had a traditional Japanese scroll and a vase of flowers in ours in *Takarazuka*. *Kuniko's* had a ship model she had made from coins.

The only furniture was a large, low table in the center. This was tipped on its side when the *futon* were put out for sleeping.

Across the front of the house and around the corner was a corridor, about three feet wide. The outside walls of the corridor were wood frames with glass panels in them. The inside partitions to the corridor were *shoji*, very thin translucent paper mounted on fragile-looking wooden frames.

The other partitions in the *tatami* rooms were *fusuma*—wooden frames with heavy opaque paper on both sides, painted with traditional designs from nature (trees, rocks, birds, etc.).

We donned slippers again to walk onto the wood floor of the hallway. At the end of the L-shaped corridor, a sink was mounted on the wall. Next to the sink was the small toilet room. The toilet was western-style (Hallelujah!) but did not flush. Instead, it was a straight drop to the septic tank below. And, of course, we changed into special toilet slippers when entering the room.

Behind our bedroom was another *tatami* room. This one had boxes stacked in it but no furniture. Narrow, steep stairs to the second floor were there.

Behind the first *tatami* room, toward the back of the house, was still another. This one held a *kotatsu* and the TV. The *kotatsu* was a low square table with a few thin cushions (*zabuton*) around it on which to sit. In the winter, a heater would be mounted under the table and a quilt placed over it to keep the warmth in. This was where the family would spend their time (a sort-of den). Fortunately there was a wall-mounted air conditioner since the weekend was unbearably hot.

On another wall of the "den" was the family altar. Each morning, food and water were placed there, a bell was rung and prayers said. Several of our gifts for *Kuniko* were placed on the altar for a time.

To the right was about a foot and a half step down into the kitchen. Since the floor was covered in vinyl, we again donned house slippers when entering. The kitchen contained a refrigerator, dish cabinets, a regular western-style kitchen table and chairs, plus a stove with a two-burner cook top, but no oven.

Sliding wooden doors with thin textured Plexiglas separated the kitchen from the wooden landing toward the front of the house. The landing then dropped down about two feet to a cement slab below. Stepping from a wooden floor to the concrete required exchanging the kitchen slippers for an outdoor pair. This space was used for storage.

At the back of this area was the bath. It might once have been outdoors before the space was enclosed. There was a step up about two feet into a tiny room where a miniscule washing machine sat next to the door. A deep Japanese-style tub (about three feet by two and a half feet by two feet deep) was squashed in the corner beside the washer. Next to the tub was a wall-mounted shower. Special slippers were again supplied to be worn in the bath-room. The partition wall separating the bath from the storeroom was wood on the bottom with textured Plexiglas above. This meant it was possible to stand in the kitchen and watch whoever was in the bath. The ceiling was so low Larry had to sit on the floor to take a shower.

As a matter of fact, all the doorways were so short he had to duck when going through them.

Upstairs were two more *tatami* rooms. One had a regular western-style twin bed. The other had a huge *kimono* chest on one wall. *Misayo, Kazue* and *Kuniko* all slept here. It also had an air conditioner.

HONORING THE ANCESTORS

Our first scheduled activity for Saturday morning was visiting the family grave. Since there was no male heir in her family, *Misayo's* husband had changed his name to *Igo*, her maiden name, and became head of the household and responsible for maintaining the monument.

The Buddhist cemetery where the family's grave marker was located was about a fifteen-minute walk from the house. First we swept around the altar, then poured water into a special hollowed-out rock in front of the upright stone carved with the family name. More water was poured over the top of the monument. And finally, a bunch of incense was lit and placed in a special hollow. Then we all clapped and the traditional prayers for *Obon* were said. We were invited to join the family, praying in our own way.

We then walked up a steep flight of stone steps to the temple building at the top of the hill, and performed the traditional hand washing, throwing of a coin, hand clapping and ringing of the bell. Prayers were said there, too.

Finally, we walked down to the Shinto shrine located below the Buddhist temple, where we threw more coins, clapped and said more prayers.

SAMURAI ENCOUNTER

After caring for the ancestors, it was time to go to the local shop and purchase the traditional summer gifts. There are two gift giving times during the year: summer and New Year. While *Misayo* selected her gifts (cases of beer and juice) and had the formal wrappings written up in proper calligraphy, we were invited by the owner to see his garden. He had a lovely little space next to the store, with a bonsai garden featuring a pond, and a large vegetable patch behind.

Then he insisted we follow him into his home. He indicated he had something he wanted to show us. To our surprise, there, on the top shelf in a storeroom, was a set of 300-year-old *samurai* armor. Larry, enamored of everything *samurai*, was enchanted.

We were escorted into his *tatami* room and served cool refreshing juice. The shopkeeper disappeared and returned in a moment with the 300-year-old *samurai* sword which went with the armor. Even *Misayo* and her mother had

179

never seen it before. He insisted we examine it closely. Then, Larry had to pose with the sword while we took pictures. We felt incredibly honored.

We were thanked several times for coming to their house. And we, in turn, bowed and thanked them for their hospitality.

OBON ODORI

That evening we attended a dance festival or *Odori*. It was held at the city hall in *Mikamo*. It reminded me of a school carnival—only much hotter.

Booths were set up selling *yakitori* (chicken on skewers), slushes, ice cream, drinks and cotton candy. One stand had toys and trinkets for the kids.

This was a real homecoming for *Misayo* and *Kazue*, so there were many friends to meet and greet. Among them was the mayor. We were introduced to him and also to the only other foreigner in town, the English teacher newly arrived from England.

The dancing began. The men's dance was lively and loosely choreographed with wildly expressive hand motions. The ladies, on the other hand, wore *kimono* and distinctive straw hats which looked like folded Mexican tacos (not to be confused with Japanese *taco* which are octopus), and danced on the toes of their *geta* (tall wooden shoes). The women danced in formation with rigidly synchronized and controlled hand motions.

One group was made up of youngsters who, had we seen them in the US, we might have thought were gang members. These were obviously the rebel group with dyed hair and piercing. Yet they performed the traditional dance with spirit, and obvious enjoyment.

There was a tiny boy of about four years old who was a great dancer. We never saw him tire the whole night.

Between the dance performances was other entertainment: *taiko* drummers, a funny samurai play, stand-up comedians and numerous drawings for prizes.

The evening ended with fireworks, and everyone—dance teams and bystanders alike—danced together for another 45 minutes. There was so much color and music and frenetic movement that it was really "over-the-top"—and it was PERFECT.

Visiting

After breakfast one day, *Kuniko* asked if we would like to visit some of her relatives since this is an important part of the *Obon* experience.

We first went to the home of Kuniko's older sister. *Shigeko-san* was a tiny stooped lady who lived with her daughter and her family in a lovely new two-story modern home. *Shigeko* spent our whole visit scurrying around bringing snacks for Larry and me. First, we had to sample her home-grown produce. Then there were all sorts of chips and candy and a homemade version of sweetened popped wheat cereal. As we were leaving, *Shigeko* scampered to her garden and picked corn, eggplant and tomatoes for us to take with us.

Next we drove to the far end of town to visit *Kuniko's* younger sister *Kinuko* or "*Kin-chan.*" She and her husband owned a little store. We were welcomed and served ice cream and cool drinks.

Kin-chan kept bringing us gifts. First was a pair of *Daruma* dolls, considered good luck. These had no arms or legs and represented a Buddhist monk who spent so much time in prayer he lost the use of his limbs. They were male and female, dressed in silk.

Next was a child's cotton coat from one of the dance teams we had seen the night before. Then she gave us fans, some with the name of their shop. They were welcome in the heat.

When we got to the car, I discovered I had an American flag fan with me. I had bought these in California and used them as decorations for 4th of July. I gave the one I had to *Kin-chan* as we left, saving face.

The last stop was at the home of *Misayo's* younger sister, *Hiromi*. Her husband, *Masataka,* raised champion *koi* (carp) fish. The year before, his fish was #1 in Japan. He showed us his prize-winners telling us some of them were worth tens of thousands of dollars. He indicated his fish tanks and said they were his bank accounts.

BIRTHDAY PARTY

Kazue had told us it would be her grandmother's birthday when we planned the trip, so we had brought a gift for her. We told *Misayo* and *Kazue* we would treat them all to dinner in thanks for their hospitality.

We walked to a nearby *yakitori* restaurant owned by *Misayo's* cousin. The food was great, and we enjoyed the evening. We all sang "Happy Birthday" to *Kuniko*, then gave her our gift. She was moved to tears.

ANOTHER FESTIVAL

After dinner, we drove into *Itami* to see the big *Obon Odori*. This was much larger than the one we had already attended. There were many more teams

181

competing, including those we had seen. They danced through the covered shopping streets in the center of town. With all the drums and flutes and strings and gongs and dancers, the cacophony was overwhelming. Judges rated each group as they went by.

It was late when we drove back to *Mikamo*. On the way, there were more fireworks. It was a fitting finale to a very special and cherished time with friends.

GOING HOME

We woke early the next morning for the long drive to *Takarazuka*. *Kuniko* was up even earlier to make tempura vegetables for breakfast as well as to take with us for lunch along with bread, fruit and *mochi*.

Kuniko gave me a beautiful fan as a gift and invited us back in October for the local harvest festival. There were hugs and tears as we departed.

We will never forget this special experience—one that few Americans get a chance to share, and I felt blessed to have made a true friend in Japan.

Golf in Japan

Ofuro (oh-fur-oh)
Japanese communal bath
It was essential to wash and rinse thoroughly outside the bath before entering the hot water for a long soak. Everyone bathed together, although, nowadays women and men usually bathe separately.

*   *   *   *   *

Larry

I never expected to experience golf in Japan. In fact I didn't even take clubs or shoes when I relocated. However, the company had other ideas. My boss, "Bowtie" Dave, organized a Facility Group Golf Tournament for the Americans and Japanese. He strongly encouraged his American team to be present. A quick call to my brother, Casey, and I was able to get a set of golf shoes FedExed from California. Fortunately, Casey and I wore the same size. The company rented clubs for those of us without them.

Clothes were another matter. Men were required to wear a sport coat or blazer to walk into the clubhouse. Shirts had to have collars, and no jeans were allowed. Dockers-type slacks were acceptable. Ties were not required. Sweaters were considered adequate attire on the course. Also, a second set of clothes was needed for changing into after the golf and bath. (Bath?) If a hat was worn, it had to be removed when entering the clubhouse. There were hat racks outside the dining room because putting headgear on the table was frowned upon. Since most of my wardrobe consisted of Hawaiian shirts and jeans, I had to dip into my pre-Universal business suit pants and jackets to find something suitable. The pants seemed tighter than I remembered.

Golf in Japan was an all-day adventure. I had to be at the course on Sunday November 26, 2000 before 8:30 a.m. So, I got up at 6:00 a.m., showered and dressed. Lorna and I headed for the *Takarazuka* station a little after 7:00 a.m. where I dropped her off. She took the train and met a friend for church and a temple sale (the Japanese version of a swap meet).

*   *   *   *   *

The *Nishinomiya-kita* Golf Course was located about fifteen kilometers (nine miles) from our home in *Takarazuka*. Since I had never been there, I allowed at least an hour for the trip. I made it in twenty minutes.

I arrived at the clubhouse where several attendants greeted the vehicle with bows. I dropped off my equipment and clothing bag at the curb, parked the vehicle, and returned to check in at the front desk. I was assigned a locker, handed the key and a folder with scorecard and chain-attached pen. (My name was already on the card.) I was directed to the locker room to change into my golf shoes, leaving my blazer and change of clothes in the locker. Then I was free to get something to eat in the dining room. There were no picture menus and no English, so a bit of hand waving and pointing got me the morning set (*say-toe*). This consisted of one piece of toast (standard Japanese double thick bread), a perfect silver dollar-sized roll of scrambled egg (pre-cooked, rolled up, sliced and served at room temperature), a small green salad with oil & vinegar & soy sauce dressing, and coffee. It was…adequate.

I met the others and found my clubs. We had a short meeting and a little warm-up on the practice putting green before tee-off. Since the abilities of the players ranged from dedicated fanatics (like "Bowtie") to first timers, we played a best ball competition or what is sometimes called a scramble. For those who don't know this system I will give a brief description.

*   *   *   *   *

Rules for Best Ball Competition

FROM THE TEE

- At each tee, all four players in a team take a shot.
- No matter how bad your shot is, you get only one try.
- When all four players have made their shots, the team plays the ball with the best lie.
- The person whose shot was the best ball is recorded.
- No team member's tee shot can be used more than sixteen times.

FROM LOCATION OF SUBSEQUENT SHOT (NOT ON GREEN)

- A tee or marker is placed at the location of the best ball.
- Each of the four team members makes a second shot from within one club length of this location (no nearer the hole).

- If the best ball landed in a bunker or the rough, the team must play from the bunker or the rough.
- The team continues in this way to the green.
- The player responsible for every best ball is recorded on every shot.

FROM LOCATION OF BEST BALL ON GREEN

- A tee or marker is placed at the location of the best ball on the green.
- Each of the four team members makes a putt from within one putter head length (+/- 4") of this location (no nearer the hole).
- The team records a team score consisting of the total number of shots taken on the hole.
- The person who hit the best shot on every stroke of each hole, including putts, is recorded.
- Every team must use at least four best balls by every player.

Now if you have all that straight, you are well ahead of where I was when we started the round. But I got the hang of it before we finished.

*   *   *   *   *

The *Nishinomiya-kita* Golf Course was new, having opened in August, 1999. Therefore, it had all the latest equipment. The attendants loaded our clubs on a small club-only cart. The cart followed a buried cable around the course while we walked. One player carried a radio control that looked like a garage door opener to start and stop the cart, which also had a direct phone to the clubhouse, extra balls, tees, towels, etc. This was a very relaxing way to play.

Out on the course, our team played the back nine (holes 10–18) first. The weather was perfect: Sunshine, very little wind and about 60°F. By the 12th hole, I took off my sweater and played in shirtsleeves. The autumn colors of the trees were magnificent, the best weather we'd had in months. Japanese courses tended to be narrow with out-of-bounds on both sides. Of note is that the course was measured in yards in spite of everything else being metric.

One member of our foursome had never hit a ball before. Another ("Bowtie" Dave) played often and hit in the high 80s. I was in the middle somewhere, not having taken a swing in the previous three years. I tried some Japanese metal woods and didn't have too much trouble hitting the ball, but my drives tended to go out-of-bounds about half the time. Fortunately, the others were there to take up the slack. In fact, one of us always managed to get a good best ball shot in. Once, our novice player even saved the day by getting a good shot to the fairway while the rest of us hit out-of-bounds. As a group, we bogeyed one, birdied one and were even par after the back nine.

Then came a long break for lunch: Curry rice and the ever-popular pork cutlet (*tonkatsu*).

*   *   *   *   *

The front nine followed lunch. I tried some older wooden drivers, and while the distance dropped, I managed to stay on the course more often. On the final hole, "Bowtie" Dave unloaded a 300+ yard drive and second shot to allow us to birdie. One bogey, two birdies on the front put us one under par for the round and the tournament winners.

After golf, we went back to the locker room.

Here life got complicated. I followed the lead of the Japanese contingent and changed out of my golf shoes and into club-provided slippers. I then took my fresh clothes to the dressing area near the bath and changed out of golf clothes there (not in the locker room as you might suppose). I placed both old and fresh clothes in a basket and set it on a shelf in the changing area. Then on to the *ofuro* (Japanese bath).

For the modest, a towel about the size of a washcloth was provided to cover private parts. Entering the bath I noticed faucets about a foot from the floor placed along one wall and small plastic seats (like footstools), pails, dippers and wash brushes nearby. Here was where we soaped-up, washed hair and rinsed until totally clean. Then we entered the bath. (Since this was a modern bath, the women had their own area.)

Upon entering the tub, it was traditional to put the washcloth/towel on top of your head to keep it dry. I followed tradition. Soaking was a group activity in Japan, like in our spa at home. It was more about socializing than cleanliness. We stayed in the tub until we were all wrinkly. Then we went back to the changing room and put on fresh clothes. After re-donning the clubhouse slippers, I returned to my locker and put on street shoes and blazer. Then I loaded all my other stuff back in the clothing bag and left it out on the shelves provided near the entry.

*   *   *   *   *

Following the bath, the group again met in the dining room for drinks and snacks (tiny fish in a walnut sauce and nearly raw meat slices for dipping in soy sauce with chopsticks, yum…). It was acceptable to hang a blazer on the back of the chair. Prizes were awarded the winners. I got a lovely *sake* set and baseball cap with the Universal Studios Japan logo.

Due to the usual Sunday evening traffic returning to *Osaka*, the fifteen-kilometer trip home took about two hours. Another character building day of golf in Japan was complete.

The Eye of the Beholder

Onsen (ohn-sen)
Hot springs used for bathing
Takarazuka was built in an area of natural hot springs.

*   *   *   *   *

Larry

Public art abounded in Japan. And much of it was not only nude, but blatantly sensual to Westerners. The Japanese had a different perception of the naked body than did American society. Perhaps it was the Shinto influence where nudity was not assigned a good or evil nature. It just was.

It didn't take us long to notice billboards and posters on the street showing extremely graphic pictures; and local Japanese TV stations routinely aired movies, soap operas and news events with full exposure, at all times of the day or night. The only taboo seemed to be the display of women's pubic hair, so occasionally that region would be blurred. But all the rest was clearly visible.

There was no shortage of naked statuary in the *Kansai* area. The city of *Kobe* was particularly noteworthy for its street art featuring Grecian-like unclothed images of both men and women on almost every corner. A twenty-five-foot-high nude depiction of *The Three Graces,* in garish gold, prominently adorned an intersection just southwest of the *Sannomiya* JR train station.

When passing through the JR *Sumiyoshi* station in *Ashiya*, one was confronted with a bas relief depicting larger-than-life-size overlapping female naked figures. Each was so anatomically correct as to leave open-jawed tourists frozen in place upon initial sighting. The subject was a little reminiscent of the famous Picasso painting *Nudes Descending a Staircase*, but reproduced in much more realistic and graphic detail. Most foreigners were quite familiar with this particular work as the station connected the JR line with the *Rokkoliner* to *Rokko* Island, the expat Mecca of the *Kansai* region.

Even our hometown of *Takarazuka* was not immune. Bracketing the bridge crossing the *Muko* River, near the *Takarazuka* Music School, were twenty-foot-high statues of naked women dancers, each standing on one foot (ala the FTD logo of the god Mercury) and upholding sticks with undulating streamers.

Lorna and I noticed that all the female statues we encountered were created in the classic Greek or Roman style. They were buxom and rounded with western features, not at all like the slimmer shape and contours typical of Asian beauty. We began to call these two friends we passed often the "*Gaijin* Nudes."

    *   *   *   *   *

In older *onsen*, communal bathing was still the norm and shared by both sexes. One just "did not notice" the other person across the pool. This could be quite embarrassing to uninitiated western tourists unfamiliar with the custom.

Modern *onsen* still featured public baths. The only difference was the segregation of the sexes. Even in these, often only a silken rope divided the areas.

We had experienced communal bathing when we attended a church weekend retreat in 1999. It was held at Camp *Sengari* in *Sanda*, about a two-hour drive from our home. Every year on the first weekend in October, the church relocated to this oasis in the mountains. Everyone helped with meals and the program. There were games, sports and activities for all ages. But one of the most anticipated events was the chance to visit the *onsen* on Saturday evening.

Families who wished to were allowed to go separately from the adults at an earlier hour. Then it was our turn.

After experiencing the whole ritual, we realized it was more of a meeting place than a place to get clean. The scrubbing and soaking were bonuses. After a few awkward minutes, we became comfortable in those strange surroundings, and the nudity ceased to be an issue.

    *   *   *   *   *

The Studio Stars Restaurant near the entrance to the park was themed to reflect the early days of film. Even though this was a cafeteria-style place and not one of the large flagship eateries, it was intended to capture the 1930s era glamour.

The centerpiece of the dining area was to be a fifteen-foot-high Art Deco sculpture of a young woman. After seeing the beautiful concept sketches produced by the art director for the venue, we were anxious to observe the finished product. The statue was installed early and well-covered for protection, while the remainder of the building was constructed around it.

During one of our weekly staff meetings, the subject of this particular statue came up on the agenda. It seemed there was a problem, not with the Japanese, but with our own USI Team. The facility was nearing completion, and the statue had, at last, been unveiled. The honchos from Florida were touring the park. When they entered the foyer, they were confronted with the image of a standing woman, head thrown back, arms uplifted, holding a platter containing an illuminated sphere. The style was Art Deco with very clean lines and smooth contours (think of the Oscar or Emmy statuette, for instance). This gave the statue an implied nude appearance. As a five- or six-foot tall person faced the fifteen-foot image, their line-of-sight fell immediately upon a particular part of the anatomy. In the vernacular of an adolescent boy, a "crotch shot."

Objections were voiced. The executives felt the presence of the statue in a family-oriented eating place with the Universal name on the door might be a bit much. The creative team, however, loved this particular piece of artwork and wanted it to stay.

The statue itself was not really the problem. The original sketches and plans showed the figure facing to the side so the profile was viewed from the doorway. However, when installed, it was oriented directly facing the entry. Maybe the Japanese obsession with symmetry and balance had struck again, or it was just a mistake. However, we would not be allowed to leave her as she was, and no one wanted to do away with her.

Suggestions to remedy the situation were quickly brainstormed. Rotating the lady was no longer an option if we wanted the restaurant to open on time. The floors were in place as were all of the adjacent fixtures. Removing her wasn't a possibility either, unless she was dismembered and destroyed in the process. She had been positioned by crane, and the building subsequently built around her. She was there to stay.

The art direction staff was in a frenzy to create a suitable camouflage for the offending area. One plan was to add a long perforated metallic strip (representing movie film) uncoiling from a film canister on the ceiling above and spiraling down and around the form, thereby carefully covering sensitive areas. However, the wide version would not bend fluidly and could not be made to look natural; and a thinner version, when applied, suggested bondage. Both were rejected.

Finally, flexible metallic mesh (like fine chain mail) was suggested for use as a clinging dress with a short draped skirt, about the length of a modern cheerleader's outfit. The mesh wasn't solid, so the underlying artwork could still be discerned on close examination.

Hurried dimensioned drawings were created; and material was purchased and fabricated. Quite a few of the team, particularly the art directors, had serious doubts about the effectiveness of this solution. However, no one could come up with a better one.

The dress finally arrived with little time to spare. The GCs fitted the garment in place, and everyone trekked, with fingers crossed, to see the results.

Even the head of the creative team was surprised and pleased with the final appearance. Still stunning, she had now taken on the aura of a graceful Degas dancer. Her new gown was an enhancement and not the detraction we had feared.

Properly clothed, our girl with the globe would now be acceptable to all.

Let the Tests Begin

SAT

Site Acceptance Tests
Operational tests run on a ride system or vehicle to assure safe
operation of the equipment under all foreseeable conditions.
These are a follow-up to Factory Acceptance Tests (FAT) for
equipment conformance to design specification.

*　　　　*　　　　*　　　　*　　　　*

Larry

Most of the time building a theme park was just hard work: meetings, decisions, and changes. Did the equipment meet the specification? Would the revised, now larger, equipment fit in the room previously designed for it? Would it work sixteen hours per day, 365 days per year? Was there enough electricity, or steam or hydraulic power, etc.? At the same time, were we still on schedule and within budget?

However, there were compensations unique to the industry. I got to play with the toys. Oops, I mean field test the rides.

Every ride system and ride vehicle had to be cycle tested for safe operation. This could involve ten thousand or more cycles of a ride vehicle around a track or course before the ride was certified. At first the vehicles contained only water-filled plastic bottles. Finally, when enough plastic bottles had survived, real people replaced them. A call went out to the team that test riders were needed at a certain time to go on this or that ride, and we became the test dummies.

*　　　　*　　　　*　　　　*　　　　*

One of my favorite tests was the "W.S.S.S.A.T" or "Water Stunt Slide Site Acceptance Test," nicknamed by the team as the "wha-zat."

In the *Peanuts* section of the park (an area based upon the Charles Shultz cartoon characters) was *Peppermint Patty's Stunt Slide*, a flume-type ride where guests in small rubber rafts slid down one of two big curving plastic tubes on a stream of water. It looked like a giant five-story Habitrail. Normally two children or one adult would fit in the raft. It was aimed at grade-school age children and would be considered tame by US water park standards.

We received a call for test riders and, since I had no meetings scheduled until after lunch and had brought a change of clothes to the office (a must during test times), I volunteered. Several of us lined up at the slide.

Each rider was expected to make a sequence of at least ten runs. My weight was taken along with other parameters such as the water level, water pump speed, inflation of the raft, etc. All this information plus the elapsed time (ET) it took to make each run from top to bottom were diligently recorded.

After a few runs, I began to know each of the two courses, not only to anticipate the turns and drops but to search for the fastest path from top to bottom. The right-hand run started quickly but made many tight turns on its descent. The left one, while starting slower, had a big drop in the middle and a very fast finish. Overall, the left course was slightly faster than the right.

Following the normal runs, several of the heavyweights (me included) were asked to make more trips to test the slides to their limits—more than 50% beyond the design parameters. I said, "Sure, why not!" Then the real fun began. Rather than one rider, we now had three (each around two hundred pounds) in a single raft along with a twenty-gallon plastic water bag. With each run, the pumps and water level were gradually increased and the raft pressure slowly deflated until it was about 20% of normal.

As the speed increased and the ET decreased, it became more difficult to stay on the raft and finish the ride. The three of us began to mold into a precision team much like the bobsled riders in the Olympics—memorizing the course and mentally seeing each turn and drop. The chant of our mantra, "Be the raft! Be the raft! Be the raft!" could be heard echoing softly through the tubes by the test staff waiting at the bottom with stopwatches.

Normal times for a run averaged twenty-two to twenty-four seconds. The fastest time for our team of three was just under seventeen seconds, a record that will stand forever—primarily because the conditions allowing such a fast time will never be duplicated during normal park operation.

The extra testing stretched into and beyond lunchtime. In fact, by the end of the test, I no longer had time to return to the office to change into dry clothes and had to go directly to my afternoon meeting. As I sat there, two puddles of water slowly spread across the floor from around the dripping pant legs of my soaked jeans. The general contractor supplied a towel, and after a good-natured laugh, the meeting continued to completion.

*　　　*　　　*　　　*　　　*

Saturday, August 25, 2000 was another unforgettable test day. Although out of the 200 or so people who were there, I was probably the only one who didn't actually see the test. On that day was scheduled the first test of a *Jurassic Park* ride vehicle plummeting down the eighty-five foot drop at the end of the ride. The test was set for Saturday, so not many people were likely to be in attendance. No announcement was made. Therefore, nearly everyone knew about it. The ride design team was there along with *Takenaka* personnel, several of the top USJ Co. brass, and anyone else who could sneak in.

The *Jurassic Park* ride vehicle, holding 25 passengers, was designed to look like a large inflatable raft similar to ones used by the military. For part of the ride, the craft actually floated on the water. However, when it came to the final drop, wheels under the boat fit into channels to lock the vehicle to the solid metal ride track. The raft accelerated to nearly sixty miles per hour on the drop and then swept into the lower lagoon. Scoops at the rear were designed to catch water and throw a lovely rooster tail some one hundred twenty five feet into the air. This effect was more than just for show as there was no other means of slowing down than the drag of the water.

Following many long discussions about how the Japanese did not like to get wet, we designed the ride in *Osaka* with a much longer run-out and landing lagoon. The idea was to let the boat skim the top of the water and slow down gradually using the rear scoops. About two-thirds of the way to the end of the landing lagoon, the boat (now traveling twenty-five miles per hour) would settle into the lagoon. The hull drag would slow it even more. The critical speed at the end of the run-out was twelve miles per hour to safely negotiate the final turn and float to the unloading ramp. If the boat slowed too quickly, the spray thrown into the air from the scoops would catch up and soak the riders (as happened in Hollywood).

The only method to adjust the slowing of the vehicle was by controlling the water level. The ride contractor calculated a preset level necessary to slow the boat to the proper speed. The ride computer would automatically stop the next vehicle before the final drop if the level varied from the preset by more than plus or minus one inch.

Controlling water level was no easy task. But it was my job to make sure everything operated correctly. A boat dropped down the waterfall every thirty seconds. This meant the sensors would determine the current level, pumps would adjust the water up or down, and the sensors confirm the correct level—all within less than thirty seconds. In addition, each boat entering the lagoon splashed some water out, lowering the level. At the same time it displaced some water in the lagoon, thus raising the level. As each was pulled onto the unload ramp, the level would drop again. Up to five boats could occupy the lagoon at one time, all of them moving and changing the calculations. To make matters worse, waves from the boat splash could affect water level sensor accuracy. And finally, the large waterfall was constantly cycling water into and out of the splashdown lagoon.

So there I sat, at 9:55 a.m. on a Saturday morning, in a basement room far under the splashdown ramp, watching the digital readouts of water level on the water control panel (in millimeters, of course, since this was Japan). In the room next door, two massive variable frequency driven water pumps (each about the size of a Volkswagen bus) hummed as they cycled makeup water through the balance tank. Outside in the lagoon, three separate sensors in different locations, hidden by rockwork, were busy signaling water level 100 times a second. The computer would compare the three sensors and determine level minus wave activity and instruct the pumps accordingly.

Lorna and the others were positioned around the splashdown lagoon.

A half hour before, the ride engineer and I had walked out onto the track in the splashdown lagoon and taken a final tape measure check of the water height, just to be sure it was correct. Now all was in readiness.

The radio crackled as the attraction manager read the checklist and we each responded.

"Vehicle ready?"

Ride engineer—"Check!"

"Track clear?"

Facility design manager—"All Clear!"

"Water level?"

(My turn)—"Water level is a go!"

"Release boat!"

Ride engineer—"9:57 a.m. Boat away!"

Even from my basement location, I could both feel and hear the rumble of the vehicle down the track. The cheers from the radio told me the landing was a success. Meter readings jumped, pumps accelerated, and within fifteen seconds the meters had returned to normal.

By the time I got outside, most of the handshakes and back-slapping were pretty well over. No one was interested in how the water level performed. It's kind of like that in my job—if I do it well, no one is supposed to notice. Only if it doesn't work do I hear about it. The day was a complete success.

*   *   *   *   *

Not all tests went perfectly. One cold winter evening after work Lorna and I stood in the back of a queue line with about two hundred others awaiting a training test for the operators at the *Backdraft* attraction. Because the floors in the building had just been polished, we were asked to remove our shoes and don paper slippers. The first fifty people went in for the initial ten-minute show segment. We watched the queue line video (in Japanese) several times. After fifteen minutes, my stocking feet in the paper slippers had gone numb. About half an hour passed before the second group of fifty was let in. More queue line video. I was beginning to not only understand the Japanese, but to recite the narration along with the voice on the video. My feet were clumps of ice. Lorna was alternately standing on one foot or the other while holding the opposite raised foot in her gloved hand in a feeble attempt at warmth. Finally after another half hour, an announcement over the PA said, "So sorry, attraction having technical difficulties, is cancelled, please come back another time."

The show was rescheduled for the following week. We were not able to attend, but heard from others it went off without a hitch. Just our luck.

*   *   *   *   *

Another test of audience stamina occurred a month later at the technical run-through for *WaterWorld*. The arena housing the show in Japan could accommodate 3000 people, so everyone—including the USJ Co. office staff, many of the construction workers, and even the site guards—was invited. We met after work at the entrance queue. For many who were not on the jobsite during the day or who were working in other areas, this was the first real view of the attraction. We stood in the queue line for about an hour while final preparations were completed inside the arena. Finally we were allowed in and found seats. Since this was a technical run-through, and not a real show, there were no actors present, no jet skis appeared, and no boats moved. We would only be seeing the mechanical "gags" (i.e. falling towers, airplane landing and pyrotechnics). This meant two seconds of excitement followed by many long minutes (where there should have been storyline) when absolutely nothing happened. Also, the show timing computer was not working correctly so the entire show (normally twenty minutes long) lasted more than an hour. It was very dark and cold by the time we finished the show.

*   *   *   *   *

One of the best perks of working in a theme park just before it opened was restaurant testing. Not only did the cooks need to be trained, so did the serving staff and managers. During the final months before soft opening (the period where sponsors, corporate management, and non-paying guests preview the park), each restaurant, food cart and stand held practice runs. And they needed hungry people to experience the service and rate the food. We were those people.

Each morning a list of the restaurants open for lunch tests that day was posted. Those of us who were interested would rush quickly to HR to get voucher tickets for our restaurant of choice. The better selections went fast. At lunchtime, we took the voucher to the designated restaurant and turned it in for the item listed on the voucher. Generally menu selections were limited to one or two items as they only prepared certain meals for the tests. But the price was right—FREE!

One day I had Italian food at *Louie's Italian Restaurant*, the next a cheeseburger, fries and cherry coke from *Mel's Diner*. One lunchtime, Lorna joined me for a chicken dinner (chicken breast, potato and salad) at the *Amity Landing Restaurant* next to the *JAWS* ride. Since, at that time, most of the food prepared in the park was "American" in style and taste, this was a treat from the normal tofu and rice faire served in the Japanese cafeteria.

Not everything went smooth though; the serving staff still had some language problems with us Americans. One day at *Boardwalk Snacks* (a fish 'n' chips place), the person ahead of me (an exceptionally tall American I will call Jasper) turned in the voucher for his meal. He held up his right hand and said, "Please hold the chips."

The young lady taking the order bowed and responded, "Hai, hai." (Meaning "Yes, yes.")

Of course, Jasper thought she understood him until they delivered him five complete dinners. We could only assume the server missed what he said and counted his fingers instead.

Since I love desserts, I think my favorite tests were the free ice cream cones at *Schwab's Drug Store*, the sundaes at *Amity Ice Cream* and the pastries at the *Boulangerie*. (Sometimes two tests were necessary for quality assurance.)

The last few months during the testing phase were eminently enjoyable, and nearly compensated for the first four years of hard work. We felt satisfaction in finally being able to appreciate the guest experience we had worked so hard to create.

Jurassic Jack

Omiai (oh-mee-aye)
An arranged Japanese marriage where the couple is introduced
*by a matchmaker (**nokoudo**). This usually takes place in a fancy*
hotel or restaurant with the couple arriving in formal dress.

*   *   *   *   *

He may have been the most beloved and best remembered member of the USJ team. He was certainly unfailingly happy—always smiling. He never complained. And whenever the strain of living in a foreign land with sometimes stranger customs became overwhelming, he provided much-needed distraction.

Jack started out as a small rubber lizard to which was attached a funny antenna ball which came from a Jack in the Box®16 restaurant in California. He looked like a white ping pong ball with a silly yellow hat, big red grin and two blue eyes.

Jack began life on the desk of one of our art directors prior to the USJ project. When the art director arrived, Jack came with him. Given Jack's resemblance to his ancestors, the dinosaurs from *Jurassic Park*, he was renamed "Jurassic Jack" and became the mascot.

The project assistant, Christiane, added a jaunty turquoise bow around his "neck," and he moved to her cubicle in the center of the group to oversee activities.

*   *   *   *   *

Shortly after our arrival in Japan, Area 3 began sending us CARE packages. The team in California made sure those of us in *Osaka* were not forgotten. Although we were miles away, we were still included. The packages contained snacks and non-perishable food like salsa and chips, candy, holiday decorations, magazines and an occasional photograph. In that first box was a picture of Jurassic Jack to post in the office.

---

16 Jack in the Box and his image are registered trademarks of Jack in the Box Inc., San Diego, CA, used with permission.

We acknowledged the receipt of the box, paying special attention to note Jack's photo. To our great surprise, the next box we received contained Jack himself. He had been relocated to Japan!

*   *   *   *   *

A new relocation coordinator had just arrived in the *Osaka* office and was appointed Jack's official liaison. She and Jack became such good friends she and her husband took him on vacation with them.

We immediately put him to work assisting in the office. When we received the prop books from Hollywood, Jack reviewed them. The rockwork models of the *JP* lagoon, New York City parks and the *JAWS* shorelines were received and assembled. Jack tested them out for scale and approved the look and feel. He did his best to help the translators and relocation team; and all the girls in the office loved him. He, of course, enjoyed the attention which came his way.

A few weeks after he arrived, one of the California relocation coordinators visited *Osaka* and identified herself as his stateside liaison. She conducted an interview to be sure he was settling in well in his new surroundings.

*   *   *   *   *

When the strain of being away from our families and trying to adjust to the new culture became overwhelming, it was not unusual for us to suggest taking Jack for a ride. As a result, he traveled over much of the country. In fact, taking Jack along became so popular he covered more of Japan than anyone else.

Most of us took photos of Jack wherever we went to send back to the Hollywood office to let them see what fun he was having.

During his stay, he visited locations not only throughout Japan, but also New Zealand, Fiji, China and *Okinawa*. His *Osaka* coordinator and her husband took Jack along on their vacation to Egypt and Africa. There are photos of Jack with elephants and with the pyramids as backdrop.

On his return to Japan from Africa, Jack nearly ran afoul of Immigration. His coordinator was carrying him in her tote bag. When it went through the x-ray machine, it was stopped and opened. She was questioned extensively about bringing foreign wildlife into the country with her. This accusation took her by surprise until she realized the silhouette of a small green lizard had shown up on the screening machine. Jack was released from the luggage and shown to the airport security folks. They weren't quite sure what to make of him, but soon determined he posed no threat to their country. Jack was allowed to return.

In his photo album were also pictures of Jack at many of the project get-togethers where he was always a welcome guest.

One of the first parties Jack attended was given by USJ Co. for a team member in town on a business trip. It was meant as chance for the USJ Co., USI and *Takenaka* teams to get to know one another. We remember it as one of the nicest parties of the project.

This was the first time most of our Japanese counterparts met Jack. At first they didn't quite understand what his role on the project was. We tried to explain, but it took a while before they accepted him. However from then on, they asked how Jack was doing and what he was doing and how he liked Japan.

As more team members relocated to Japan, Jack became even more in demand. And after January 1999 when we moved to the jobsite, Jack tended to move around. He was often waiting in the cubicle of the latest expat to greet them when they arrived.

*   *   *   *   *

After he had been in Japan for a while, a group was returning to Hollywood for their home leaves and asked if Jack would like to accompany them. Since he feared flying alone, he was quite agreeable to joining them. His grin was wide as he departed. There was a party to welcome him home, and everyone stopped by to say hello. However, when his week in California was over, he was happy to return to *Osaka*.

In fact, after being in Japan for some time, he indicated he was feeling very much at home there and might like to stay. All the young girls on the project made a fuss over him and called him "cute." This was very appealing to him.

The team discussed his request to remain in Japan after the completion of the project, and agreed that, if it was his wish, we'd support him. Plans began to find him a permanent job in the show for *Jurassic Park*. It was, after all, where he truly belonged.

*   *   *   *   *

Meanwhile, the senior show producer for Area 3 arrived and agreed that Jack's wishes to remain should be honored. But she also believed he should not be left in the country by himself. So the search for his bride began.

Several months later—near the end of the project—a suitable bride-to-be was found. She was quite traditional, but also somewhat modern. She seemed to embody the qualities that appealed to Jack. She was always smiling, never complained, somewhat resembled him, but was clearly Japanese. (Her dark hair and eyes were a hint as well as the fan she always carried with her.) Her name was Junko. ("June" for short.)

Finally, the evening of the Project Completion party, an "*omiai*" (formal introduction) was arranged. His *Osaka* relocation coordinator, dressed in formal *kimono*, once again served him well by acting as the go-between. The rest of the team members were delighted to know Jack would not remain in Japan alone, and he seemed very pleased with his proposed bride. During the entire evening of the party, they just grinned at each other. It was obviously a love match.

The team arranged for the couple to have a permanent home in the "ruined" control room in the *JP* show where their friends could catch a glimpse of them while on the ride. Most of us had to leave before the sets were completed, but were confident that Jack and "June" would be spending their lives happily engaged in entertaining the guests who braved the *Jurassic Park* adventure.

*   *   *   *   *

Some time later, a few of the original team members returned to Japan to assist in creating a new attraction in the park. One of their early visits was to *JP* where they tried to spot Jack and "June." They reported they were unable to see them while on the ride.

Finally, one of the team members entered the control room where they were supposed to have been…They were gone.

Those of us who had enjoyed their company during our participation on the project were at first very sad to think they were no longer at the park. It had been reassuring to know we would find the pair living happily in *JP* if we ever returned to *Osaka*.

However, we have become a bit more philosophical. We are grateful for all the happy memories we shared with Jack. And we wish them well—wherever they are now. We all hope that they have chosen to live anonymous lives somewhere in Japan raising little "Jacks" and "Junes." Perhaps the fame just became too much for them…

Final Celebrations in Japan

Kampai (camp-aee)
Empty cup—used as the most common form of toast in Japan

*　　　*　　　*　　　*　　　*

Lorna

The time had come to experience the closing events of the project and of our sojourn in Japan.

Sayonara Party

Our holiday celebrations began on December 15, 2000 when we attended the Sayonara Party given for the entire project team including the GCs, USJ Co., and the USI (American) team members.

The evening began with numerous speeches and toasts celebrating the success of our efforts. Glasses were raised and the cry of, "*Kampai*" echoed through the building. The park was nearly complete. There had been no lost time accidents. We were under budget and ahead of schedule. "*Kampai*" indeed!

The meal was a typical Japanese-style stand-up buffet dinner prepared by the USJ Food Services team. The choices were good and plentiful with both Japanese and American dishes. Larry was ecstatic because there was a large dessert selection. (The first Japanese word he learned was *desarto*, pronounced "de-zaa-toe.")

The first entertainer of the evening was a classical Japanese dancer accompanied by music played on traditional instruments. It was one of the few times we experienced this art form.

The second half of the program featured a pianist, plus a small orchestra and two singers. They began with classical pieces, then moved to American standards and ended with Christmas music. By then, some of the folks had freely imbibed of the champagne, *sake*, beer, wine and whatever else was being served. A few of the Japanese started dancing and invited others to join them.

In a culture where dancing is not encouraged, this came as quite a surprise. They must have spent too much time around the Americans.

It was a lovely event, and we all felt the sense of celebration in the air.

Christmas Concert

Our friend *Yoshida-san* from *Takenaka* gave us tickets for a Christmas concert on the 21st. We were very touched that he had thought of us. In traditional end of year Japanese gift giving, gifts are given from the bottom up—meaning gifts are given only to those in a higher position, not the other way around. *Yoshida-san* was quite elevated in the *Takenaka* organization and outranked both of us put together. It was a sign of our friendship with him that he chose to give the tickets to us. The other recipients were a director and a Vice President.

The performer was a countertenor named Slava. (Countertenors are male singers who perform in the soprano range.) He had a wonderful voice and performed with a pianist and chamber orchestra.

Project Wrap Party

The Project Wrap Party, a sit-down dinner for the USI team, was held the following evening at the *Kobe* Bay Sheraton Hotel. We were each awarded what we called "Unis." (You know about the Oscar and Emmy…) The "Uni" was a trophy-like statuette featuring the Universal globe, the flags of the US and Japan and an engraved brass plaque with our names and departments on them. Each one was individually awarded by the department directors.

Photo Opportunity Day

On Saturday, the 23rd, all the families of the people who worked on the project were invited to spend several hours in the park taking pictures. A few attractions were open: *Motion Picture Magic, Animation Celebration, Backdraft* and some of the Snoopy area. It was a thrill to see people enjoying the park for the first time. Many of the GC, USI and USJ employees brought their families. The kids loved the *Peanuts* area as we had hoped they would.

We spent most of our time locating and photographing windows. The names of all the people who worked on the project for USI were displayed on signs and the upper windows of buildings throughout the park. Our names were on the same façade in the New York area. Doc's Candy Store was on the corner, and around to the left of that, we could be found. Larry's window was on the 2nd floor as a bail bondsman, and mine was on the 3rd floor as a tailor. (Check it out if you are ever in the park.)

As we strolled along the Main Lagoon behind the Discovery Center restaurant in the *Jurassic Park* area, we encounter Berj and his family.

"Who would have thought on that day in 1998 when all of us traveled to *Kobe* for our alien registrations, we'd be standing here today?" Larry asked.

"Yes," Berj replied. "I can remember saying this was a very difficult site, and we'd never be able to get the soil improved enough to sustain plant life. Now look at it."

And we did. It was more beautiful than our dreams and hopes for it could ever have been.

Piano Recital

We had to leave the park early to get to the piano recital for our neighbor *Kazue's* piano students. She had specially invited us to attend. During the previous week I had baked five cakes. (Quite a challenge considering they were baked in our one-cubic-foot-sized convection oven, a layer at a time.) Before leaving that morning, I also baked two of *Auntie Wanda's Pumpkin Pies*.

We arrived just as the recital began. It was fun watching the kids (some as young as three or four) performing. Afterward, we shared a huge meal. *Misayosan* must have cooked for days to prepare the rest of the food. We were surprised to discover nearly half the parents spoke some English.

After the meal, *Kazue* played for everyone. Her second piece was "Rustle of Spring," a piece she had nicknamed "Vera's Song" in honor of my mother. Her last selection was "Le Rhone." This beautiful number was written by a talented Japanese composer named *Hattori* when he was only fourteen. One of our Japanese "kids," *Ikue*, had played it for us when she was in California in the spring of 1998. I had asked *Kazue* if she knew it. She subsequently learned the piece, and played it once again in our honor.

Then she asked me to play "White Christmas" while the parents and students sang—in English. They had learned the song as a surprise for us.

Kazue had asked us to help her conclude the recital with a candlelight service. We passed out candles and explained (with *Kazue* translating) how many Christian Christmas Eve services end with the lighting of candles and the singing of "Silent Night." *Kazue* played the song, and we started lighting the candles. It was very moving.

*   *   *   *   *

Christmas Eve

At 5:00 p.m. we picked up *Kazue* to attend the Christmas Eve service with us. This would be her first experience in a Christian church.

It was a lovely service—different from the ones we have enjoyed with the congregation in California—but most enjoyable nevertheless.

At the end of the evening, we were invited to join in a sing-along of the "Hallelujah Chorus" from Handel's *Messiah*. *Kazue* joined us and really enjoyed herself. Since she is a concert pianist, she can sight read much better than we, and was easily able to follow the music.

To our delight, and hers, the service ended with the lighting of candles and the singing of "Silent Night."

On the way home in the car she said it was the best Christmas Eve she had ever spent.

Christmas Day

We had eight for dinner on Christmas afternoon. *Kazue* and *Misayo-san* came as did our friends Nicole, Kit, Kathy and Casey.

We served turkey and dressing, mashed potatoes, peas, and a specialty of one of our favorite California restaurants—mixed frozen fruit served with sparkling cider. *Misayo-san* brought *o-sushi* (vinegar rice with egg served in a dish rather than rolled) and some New Year's *mochi* (sweet pounded rice with red bean paste inside). Kit and Kathy brought a salad and fudge, and we had pumpkin pie and trifle for dessert.

Kazue and *Misayo-san* had never tried fudge before. When they were offered a piece, they each took a bite. From the looks on their faces one might have suspected they were encountering something very bitter. But it was much too sweet for their taste.

*   *   *   *   *

Although we would rather have been home in the US for Christmas, we felt we had been blessed by our celebrations in Japan. And we were looking forward to spending the New Year in California.

Closure

Sayonara
Good-bye

*   *   *   *   *

Lorna

Our last week in Japan brought to mind the old saying, "What goes around, comes around." Our final days there felt like the closing of circles.

*   *   *   *   *

Larry's first trip to Japan was in February of 1998. Now exactly three years later we were preparing to depart. On the first night of that now long ago trip, on the hotel pillow next to the courtesy chocolate mint, Larry found a card with a Japanese *haiku* message. He, of course, had eaten the chocolate, but for some reason had also saved the card. In his final email, announcing his departure from the project, thanking the team and wishing them all the best, Larry had scanned and attached the card and its message saved for so long. The *haiku* was translated:

At my Departure in Spring
Birds Cry and the Eyes
Of Fishes are Filled with Tears

To Larry, it summed up his mixed feelings: the joy of returning home to California and the sadness in the departure and separation from the friends made during our stay.

*   *   *   *   *

We had begun our working lives in Japan on the 28th floor of the *Osaka* World Trade Center. We ended our stay in a room on the 28th floor of the Ritz Carlton Hotel in the city.

Our first Japanese daughter, *Yuka*, had met us at the airport when we arrived. On the Sunday before we left, we had tea at the Ritz with her. She had just begun working for the Operations Division of USJ Co. in the park. It felt as though we were passing responsibility for our creation on to her.

      *   *   *   *   *

When we first saw our apartment, it was new and had no window coverings except large sheets of paper. Mrs. K. was responsible for providing the draperies as well as our appliances. She emailed us photos of busy patterns and colorful designs. We rejected them all. Then we asked her to find some solids, and we picked the closest match to the gray color of the carpeting. It was the perfect choice since the floor-to-ceiling windows were twelve feet tall, and the huge curved surface was nearly sixty feet long. When the drapes were closed, attention was drawn toward our artwork and furniture inside the room. And when they were open, the spectacular view demanded attention. We enjoyed them throughout our time there.

However, on Friday, February 24, 2001, after our last night spent in the apartment, the people who were purchasing all the used Japanese furniture and appliances arrived to collect the refrigerator, air conditioners, light fixtures and draperies. We both felt sad seeing the windows bare once again. At that moment, the place really ceased to be "home."

      *   *   *   *   *

On Saturday the 25th, moving day, our friend *Misayo-san* came to our apartment after she finished her own work at *Burger City*. She carried rags and an apron, and worked hard to help us finish the scrubbing and dusting. She saved us lots of time, and we were able to close up right after the movers left.

We had heard horror stories of problems people experienced during the final walkthrough inspections of their apartments. We were told Japanese landlords were much more critical than American ones. So we made sure our place was immaculate. We literally backed our way out the door waxing the wood floor in the hall after the movers left. The next day, we met the inspector, building manager and a translator there. The inspector spent less than five minutes looking through the place, opening closet doors and checking for cleanliness, then pronounced, "No damage."

After the inspection, we walked down to "Papa" and *Misayo-san's* apartment. There were a few snow flurries on the way down the hill, reminding us we would be happy to be leaving the bitter *Osaka* winters.

On the day we selected our apartment in May of 1998, we had stopped at *Burger City* on our way to the airport. There we met *Akira* ("Papa") and *Misayo-san* for the first time. As *Misayo-san* said, "It was an instant heart connection."

When we arrived at their home for the last time, she made us a cup of tea, just like our first meeting.

At last it was time for our hardest good-bye. I cried. *Misayo-san* cried. *Kazue* cried. And it was just as painful as all of us had anticipated. "Papa" insisted on driving us to the train station. *Kazue* came along, but *Misayo-san* wasn't up to another tearful farewell. Neither was I.

*   *   *   *   *

On Tuesday morning, February 27th, we went down to the buffet breakfast at the hotel for the last time, where we were joined the former project assistant for Larry's area, Christiane. When we first arrived in the country, she sent us CARE packages and emails and reminded the folks in Hollywood we were still around. Because of her, the Area 3 team remained cohesive. She was still working on the USJ project, but with the group coordinating corporate sponsorship. We said good-bye hoping to see her again when she returned to Hollywood in mid-March.

After we checked out of the hotel, we took the train to USJ for the last time. It was an unexpected gift. We had assumed my last language class and Larry's last day of work would be our final times at the park. But we were not comfortable sending our important documents, bankbooks and IDs through the mail to the office, even though it was Japan and should have been perfectly safe. We had one last opportunity for hugs and farewells with those remaining. And we got the chance to purchase a few USJ logo items.

One of our regrets had been the lack of availability of items with the new park's logo. However, our last day in Japan happened to be when the employees who would be working in the shops were trained. More importantly, they needed to know how to handle employee discounts. So, for the final time, we were able to take advantage of one of the best perks of working for the company. Our timing was incredible, since this was the only day this particular training was conducted prior to park opening. I was finally able to buy a USJ sweatshirt. And Larry got his T-shirt.

We had turned in our IDs and were passing the park entrance on our way to the train station, when we met *Setsuko-san* and *Mukai-san* emerging after their shopping spree. These were two of the first people we met when we arrived at the office in the *Osaka* World Trade Center in 1998. *Setsuko-san* had been the administrator for the local relocation team at the time, and *Mukai-san* was the office manager. Somehow, it seemed fitting that they were the last Universal people we saw as we departed.

* * * * *

On Larry's first visit to the apartment where we would live in *Takarazuka*, he met Kenny Hill who was a director of the Ritz Carlton Hotel. He was the only other foreigner living in our building. On the last day the movers were loading our furniture (Saturday), Kenny's wife Erika and daughter Jessica brought us lunch. As we were walking out the door after the cleaning was finished, Erika arrived again as if she sensed we were about to go.

Kenny often left for work about the same time we did each day, and whenever he was waiting at the bus stop as we were going out the driveway, we gave him a lift to the station. On this day, Erika offered to drive us into town to catch the train. Riding down the hill with Erika reminded us of the many morning trips we had made with Kenny.

When we returned to the hotel following our last trip to the park, Erika and her children, Andy and Jessica, were waiting for us. They had come to say good-bye. We had received a call from Kenny the night before saying they would be there, so we had gotten each of the kids a little USJ gift. And somehow it seemed just right that we had been met on our arrival in Japan by a friend, and we would be leaving saying good-bye to friends. Kenny came out to join his family as we boarded the shuttle bus. Our last view was of the four of them waving good-bye as we left for the airport.

The circle was closing, and we were headed home.

We Did It!

Gomi (Gō -mē)
Trash. This was placed in the designated bin on designated days,
sorted and wrapped as specified.

*　　　*　　　　*　　　　*　　　　*

Lorna

Although occasionally it seemed as though our time was spent in disagreement and misunderstanding, the US and Japanese teams worked surprisingly well together—despite the cultural differences. We adapted to the Japanese meeting style, and they bent to some of our business practices as well.

In the end, we created an outstandingly beautiful place ahead of schedule and under budget—the first theme park to accomplish it.

One of our favorite quotes is:

"The greatest enemy of creativity is unlimited resources."[17]

USJ proved it.

*　　　*　　　　*　　　　*　　　　*

During the early days of USJ, Universal Studios was completing Universal Islands of Adventure in Florida. Overruns and delays caused the project to go over budget. To complete that park and start generating income, Universal Studios made the decision to reduce funding for USJ. Those cuts forced the design teams to be more creative in their approach to the new park.

For previous locations, each attraction had been assigned one facility design manager (FDM), project architect and project engineer (PE). But in Japan, only one of each was assigned to a whole area, comprised of several facilities. There were times when the people in those positions felt stretched beyond their limits.

The project was still being staffed when we moved to Japan, so Larry spent several months acting as PE for both Areas 3 and 4. He tried to attend as many

---

[17] Author unknown

meetings as possible and to keep the Hollywood team apprised of decisions being made.

We worked with some of the best art directors and show producers in the business. They were very resourceful, and whenever requested materials were not available, they'd find other, and often better, solutions. The overall look and feel of the park owed a great debt to their vision. They, too, had far more responsibility than on previous assignments.

*   *   *   *   *

The GCs had never created faux rockwork previously and were excited to learn how. Our rockwork consultant and his staff made it fun for everyone.

The translators especially enjoyed working with this group. The process was interesting, creative and very different from most of their other translation assignments. The work was performed on the site and not in a conference room. And the individual sculptors were easy to work with. Whoever was slated to translate for this activity had the choice assignment for the day.

In addition to the sculptors who created the rockwork throughout the park, the scenic painters' skills were awesome. Once the rockwork and buildings were in place, it was the job of the scenic painters to transform the basic shapes into the desired elements through skillful application of paint. We remember the day the first building along the wharf was completed, and we rode our bicycles across the site to see it. There it stood—an aged shack with "peeling" and faded paint. It looked perfect, and we knew the final look of the buildings was in competent hands.

*   *   *   *   *

One of Larry's favorite tasks was designing a wave maker for the entrance pool of the *WaterWorld* show—with no budget. There was a small pool across the entrance to the arena. At night, lights around the perimeter cast reflections of the water onto the walls. But it needed to move to mimic the ocean tides. It originally resembled a small swimming pool or lake.

He first requested the GC to add a bent section to the supply pipe re-circulating water into the pool so it would pour from above rather than flow in below the surface. This alone caused some movement of the water. Then he headed for the *gomi* (trash) pile.

When a significant number of Universal employees and vendors had arrived at the site, it became apparent some sort of transportation would be needed to convey them from place to place. Some old bicycles were purchased. They could be borrowed from one area and ridden to another. Often they were abandoned throughout the park which made it convenient to grab one to get around.

After a time, many people began buying their own personal bikes. And, as the tires went flat and things broke on the used ones, the remains were thrown in a pile. Occasionally the parts from one were used to fix another, but for the most part, it was a trash heap. In fact, the whole bunch was disposed of at the end of the project.

For his wave maker, Larry took one of the old broken bicycles from the junk pile and removed the tires. Next he purchased coffee from the vending machines for a couple of weeks. (In Japan, coffee came from the machines hot and in cans the size of soda cans, but about half as large in diameter.) Then he found some old water bottles lying around the site. Finally, he located some chain in another scrap pile.

Since some of the props for the *WaterWorld* show were being painted, he set his "*gomi*" bike in the overspray and it was given the same aged look as the rest of the props. Next, he cut the coffee cans in half, bent them up to make them look worn and screwed them to the bike rim. The water bottles were filled with dirty water, sealed and attached to the peddles on the chain. Finally, this contraption was anchored to the stadium wall with the coffee-canned rim in the stream from the pipe. This created a waterwheel effect. As the wheel turned, the peddles rotated causing the water bottles to go up and down, creating turbulence in the water. It looked aged and cool and the ripples reflecting on the arena walls at night were very effective. Best of all, it was free!

*   *   *   *   *

Sometimes, however, things appeared that were too nice to use as they were.

In the *WaterWorld* show, the platforms in the water were surrounded by old tires as bumpers for the boats and jet skis used in the show. The GCs were shown sketches of the designs and photos of the Hollywood set. Some had even visited California and seen it for themselves.

The tires arrived and were installed. Then the Area 3 team went to the arena to look at the sets. There were the tires—brand new tires—neatly spaced and aligned perfectly around the platforms. It was another case of Japanese precision and desire for only the best flying in the face of the organized chaos intended. It seemed positively criminal to beat up and put ragged holes in perfectly good new tires in order to create the required look. But it was done, and some were repositioned in a more haphazard manner around the platforms. In the end, the effect we were after was achieved.

*　　　*　　　*　　　*　　　*

The GC construction team, most of whom had never seen San Francisco, New York, New England, Hollywood or any of the other American sites recreated in the *Osaka* park, built amazingly convincing replicas of these areas. Their precision allowed us to complete the park without a single day of lost time due to accidents. And the park opened on March 31, 2001, one day earlier than originally scheduled.

Each of the GCs brought to the project many years of experience and an enthusiasm we had rarely seen. And while there were often lapses in translation and misunderstandings, in the end when we could finally enjoy the completed park, there was only one way to describe it—AWESOME!

*　　　*　　　*　　　*　　　*

In its first year of operation, Universal Studios Japan broke all previous theme park records. This was from *Variety* on March 5, 2002:

=======================================
JAPAN
=======================================
U park draws 10mil

Universal Studios Japan theme park passed the 10 million visitor mark Sunday, just 11 months after opening, beating Tokyo Disneyland's 1984 record of 9,933,000 visitors in its first year.

Fewer Japanese have traveled overseas since last fall, opting for domestic attractions instead. USJ's first-year goal was 8 million visitors.

Post Script

Lorna

We were back, but we weren't the same people who left. We had a new appreciation for small things like wide traffic lanes, discount stores, choices, freeways and an abundance of English-language TV. There were things we missed: public transportation, a constant sense of safety, our million dollar view and, most of all, our friends. And there were things we didn't miss such as the extreme heat and cold weather, humidity, typhoons, narrow roads, getting lost, deep ditches and not always understanding the language.

We were happy to be back in our home in Dana Point with our friends and family. Larry was delighted to be near the beach again and able to go surfing much more often.

Touches of Japan can be found throughout our home, little reminders of that special time in our lives. My dolls and Larry's ninja sword are displayed in our "Japanese" room. It doesn't have *tatami* on the floor, but it does have our Japanese scroll (*kakejiku*) on the wall with seasonally changed artwork. The pins and other mementos we collected are framed in a shadowbox, and Larry's golf award *sake* set is on display.

My prized *kimono* from *Kyoto* hangs on our entry wall, adorned with a beautiful *obi*, a farewell gift from *Misayo-san*.

Both of us came full circle at work. Larry was unemployed only one week before he accepted the same job he was prepared to take the day Universal called in 1997. And in the spring of 2002, my previous employer called to ask if I was interested in returning to the position I had held prior to leaving for Japan.

Larry lunches on *sushi* at least once a week. He's convinced his coworkers it's a basic food group. We both maintain our chopstick prowess—just in case...

We still miss being part of the USI team. Larry often speaks fondly of his time with the dinosaurs and sharks. He would love another opportunity to work in that crazy and exciting environment. So would I.

He has managed to get several small assignments inspecting and testing rides in the entertainment industry for that other Southern California theme

215

park giant. But it's not as satisfying as being immersed in the process from concept to completion.

Losses

Some of the most difficult things to deal with while we were away were the losses of close friends and family members. We became acutely aware of how much the shared rituals of closure helped to channel the grief. My way of coping was to write about the person, then email the piece back home. I was later told several of these were read during memorial services. It made me feel a little more connected, but we still felt most isolated at those times.

Raouf was the first loss on the project, but not the last. In August 2000, the Area 3 show producer's husband died in Japan. We had enjoyed them as a couple, and felt his absence keenly. She chose to stay and complete her responsibilities. We hoped keeping busy would help ease her transition to being single again.

In August 2001, *Kazue Igo* visited us for several weeks. We showed her all the Southern California sights, and spent a long weekend in San Francisco where her father had visited many years earlier. She fell in love with the city just as he had. On December 12, 2001, *Akira Igo* ("Papa") died in an automobile accident in *Osaka*. We were profoundly saddened at the loss of yet another precious friend.

Then in June 2003, we lost one of the younger members of the team to cancer. His death came as a tremendous shock and reminder that everyone who worked on the project left a little piece of themselves with the rest of us.

The Team

Since most of the team members were on contract only for the duration of the project, they left Japan and disbursed like the petals on a cherry tree in a brisk wind. They're now scattered throughout the world.

We stay in touch with quite a few and are always happy to hear from them. We also maintain a website for the group where we can keep everyone up-to-date on the latest happenings.

At last count, there were at least ten weddings among team members. Children have been born as well. And we have received their photos.

In 2002, some members of the original design team returned to *Osaka* to participate in the construction of the *Spiderman* attraction. It opened in January 2004 and has drawn record numbers to the park again.

We continue to hope the park, to which we devoted several years of our lives, will bring joy to generation after generation of guests. That, after all, is why we did it.

Acknowledgments

We would like to especially thank the following who made this book possible:

❖ *Lagunita Writers' Group*—Julie, Margie, Sheila, Maria, Christie, Steve, Len & Lu, Lois, and especially Martha. Your encouragement, suggestions and gentle criticism led to a much more interesting manuscript. Your input was invaluable, and your friendships are treasured. Oh, and thanks for struggling through all the Japanese!

❖ *Pat*—It's all your fault! Beginning with that first phone call, you launched us on a journey into the strange and wonderful world of theme park construction. Thanks—we think. We sincerely appreciate your friendship, support, generosity and loving "nagging." Without you, we never would have completed the work. And thanks for allowing your family (Bruce and Tracy) to become our family. We love you all.

❖ *Stephen, "Bowtie" Dave, Cathy, Casey, Berj, Fraser, "Jurassic Mark," Mike, Stresh, the "Nihon Cowboy" and all the rest of the gang*—Thanks for reading the very rough drafts, filling the holes in our memories with yours, and for encouraging us to tell the story. It's your story too. Thanks for sharing the adventure with us! (A special 'thank you' to Stephen for being a packrat and unearthing the original April Fools' email.)

❖ *Kim*—Not only do we love you because you are our daughter, but your keeping things going at home in California made it possible for us to complete the project. You are a loving and special person, and we're glad you're ours!

❖ *Kay*—Your suggestions and wisdom made a huge difference during our Japanese sojourn. We treasure your friendship.

❖ *The folks at KUC*—Kobe Union Church was our life raft during the early days in Japan. There we discovered a church family who kept us going with love, encouragement and practical help. God bless you all.

❖ *Our CPC family*—Our church family in California at Community Presbyterian Church of San Juan Capistrano also encouraged us with email messages. Nearly every day one or more of our brothers or sisters in faith sent us a missive. We were reminded that we were not forgotten.

More importantly, your prayers were felt and appreciated more than you will ever know.

❖ *Universal Studios*—For making it all a reality.

Lorna would like to thank

❖ *Larry*—You are my dearest love, my best friend and my soul mate. I'm so glad I chose you and you chose me. We have had richer experiences and a life more wonderful than I could ever have dreamed. But I would have been happy just to share whatever time I had in this life with you. Thanks for always making me laugh and telling me you love me. That's the most important thing of all!

Larry would like to thank

❖ *Lorna*—Thank you for putting up with a guy who said "this experience might be fun" before even considering the full impact. For giving up a wonderful job and traveling nine thousand miles so we could be together. For keeping our finances solvent in both yen and dollars. For creating a bit of home even while in a foreign land. I love you so very much.

978-0-595-34584-7
0-595-34584-0

Printed in the USA
CPSIA information can be obtained
at www.ICGtesting.com
LVHW072137190923
758756LV00027B/182

9 780595 345847